Make Money with Guns

How to get your FFL and become an SOT

Ryan M. Cleckner

RocketFFL, LLC

ROCKETFFL

RocketFFL.com

5543 Edmondson Pike Nashville, TN 37211

Print ISBN: 978-0-9994173-5-5

DISCLAIMER: This publication contains content intended to educate readers about obtaining their federal firearms license. Although the topics are legal in nature and the author is an attorney, nothing in this book is legal advice and no attorney-client relationship exists. This book is for information only and readers must confirm all information prior to relying upon it.

Contents

INTRODUCTION

My name is Ryan Cleckner and I am a former special operations sniper, university professor, bestselling author, and an attorney that specializes in firearms law – specifically the federal laws and regulations governing the firearms industry.

I have been working in the firearms industry since 2010 – I have managed federal government affairs for the trade association for the firearms industry (NSSF), I have been a Vice President at Remington Outdoor Company, a SAAMI board member, I co-founded and operated GunUniversity.com, FFLSafe.com, and more, and I've taught people how to get their Federal Firearms License (FFL) through an online course at RocketFFL.com since 2017.

In that time, RocketFFL.com has helped over 20,000 people get their FFL and set it up the right way to avoid trouble with the Bureau of Alcohol, Tobacco, Firearms, and Explosives (ATF). As an attorney, I have also represented hundreds of clients (retailer, manufacturer, and importer/exporter FFLs) across the country against the ATF and have testified in Congress, multiple times, about and against the ATF.

I have resisted putting this information into a book for almost 10 years now because an online course allows me to keep the information up-to-date. However, too many of you have asked for a book that you can keep on your shelf to reference and, to that end, here we are. Please note that this information is accurate at the time of printing – I can not know nor guarantee the future.

Therefore, I have created a spot on RocketFFL.com for this printing/edition of this book where you can see any and all updates. I also intend to update this book as often as is necessary to ensure that I am providing the most accurate information possible.

This would be a great time to check the website to make sure that the book you're holding is up-to-date.

Check this book's status and/or updates and also find links to extra information at this URL (or QR Code): https://rocketffl.com/book1

Chapter 1

How to Use This Book

Welcome to your new future as an FFL!

You're making the first big step in getting, and maintaining, your FFL the *right* way! A congratulations are in order - taking the time to learn about how to do this the right way shows that you are taking this process seriously and you are now officially much more likely to succeed!

Too many folks try to do this on their own and are setup for failure because they don't know what they don't know. I have many clients who are good people and who want(ed) to do things right but they ended up in trouble with the ATF during their first compliance inspection because they did the right things in the wrong way.

I look forward to having you in our industry.

In this chapter, we're going to cover:

- **What to expect from this book**
- **Organization of materials**
- **How to use this book to get your FFL**
- **Summary of the book**

What to expect from this book

This book will walk you through every step of the process to getting your own FFL – it will also give you a bit of an education, too. You'll learn the background of some requirements and you'll receive some basic compliance training as well.

Mid-way through the fifth section of this book, Basic Firearm Compliance, you're most likely going to realize that you need more compliance training. That's ok! I've linked resources for more compliance training in the URL/QR Code in the Introduction section – there's way to much information on compliance to include on a book that is made to help you get your FFL.

This book is NOT legal advice. Yes, I'm a lawyer. Yes, you're relying on me to give you accurate information. However, no attorney/client relationship exist as a result of you reading this book. If you'd like to form an attorney/client relationship because you'd like to be covered should anything ever happen, or if you someday end up in trouble and need attorney support, you can find ways to contact me and hire me as your personal firearms lawyer through this book's information by following the URL/QR code in the Introduction section.

Organization of materials

This book is divided into distinct sections, each with their own chapters.

I have organized the information to give you a solid foundation of information before you start to fill out your application.

Please be patient - the information will likely help guide some of your decisions and answers on the application.

How to use this book

You should work through this book from beginning to end without jumping around from chapter to chapter (at least the first time through). After you've completed the book, you are welcome to come back and review any chapter if you're anxious waiting for the ATF to approve your paperwork and you'd like to read something again.

Summary

This book has 8 sections:

1. Introduction

2. Individual Requirements

3. Business/Entity Requirements

4. Application

5. Basic Firearm Compliance

6. Initial ATF Inspection

7. Receipt of FFL

8. Becoming an SOT

If you look at those, you'll notice that only one of these sections focuses on the FFL application itself. This is because there's a bit of background for you to learn before you can make the right decisions concerning your new license.

There's a lot of benefit to an FFL, but there's also a lot of responsibility – you need to make the right decisions now to start off on the right foot. After the application is complete and submitted, there are four more sections to read – DON'T SKIP THESE! Three of the final sections will introduce you to basic firearms compliance, help get you ready for your first inspection with the ATF (yes, it's coming), and get you started operating as an FFL. The fourth section will help you determine if you want to become an SOT, and how.

Section summaries

1 – Introduction. This section covers how to use this book (what you're reading now), what to expect throughout the book, and it will give you a basic background of the FFL system and a discussion of the different types of FFLs (including which will be best for you).

2 – Individual Requirements. This section explains who may possess an FFL and it explores who else may need to meet the same requirements as you and also be listed on your FFL. For example, if you have an employee who will have some control over "firearms operations," then they will need to be listed on your license as well.

3 – Business/Entity Requirements. This section will help you understand some of the business-specific decisions you need to make and business-related requirements that you'll need to follow. For example, it will explore the need to intend to be "engaged in the business" of firearms and also describe location and hours of operation requirements. *NOTE: the "location" chapter might very well be the toughest chapter with which you'll need to comply.*

4 – Application. Here's the paperwork. This section will help you fill out your application, step-by-step, and gather all of the required materials with checklists. There's a lot to do, but I make it as painless as possible.

5 – Basic Firearm Compliance. While you're waiting on your application to process, you're going to want to study this section. This is a brief overview of the MANY firearm laws and regulations.

6 – Initial ATF Inspection. Before you even start day-one as an FFL, you're going to have an "initial inspection." An Industry Operations Investigator (IOI), not an agent,

will meet with you to ensure that you understand your requirements and to confirm that some of the basic requirements have been met. Don't panic – I give you everything you'll need to know. In fact, you'll be so ready for this inspection that you shouldn't be surprised if you end up teaching the IOI about their own requirements/job.

7 - Receipt of FFL. This section starts you off on the right foot the day you receive your FFL.

8 – Becoming an SOT. This section helps you understand what an SOT is, whether you'll want to become one, and how.

Chapter 2

Background

In this chapter, we're going to cover:

- **Firearms laws and regulations**
- **FFL licensing system**
- **Required intent**
- **Categories of firearms**

Firearms laws and regulations

There are many laws and regulations which govern the manufacture, import/export, sale, and possession of firearms. The major laws are the National Firearms Act of 1934 (NFA), the Gun Control Act of 1968 (GCA), and the Arms Export Control Act (AECA). The major regulations are ATF's firearm regulations, the International Traffic in Arms Regulations (ITAR), and the Export Administration Regulations or EAR - note, the abbreviation for ITAR is said as a word (EYE-tar) whereas EAR is spelled out (E. A. R.). If you say EAR (rhymes with hear) when you're referring to the E-A-R, you're going to get some funny looks.

If you're wondering what the difference between a law and a regulation is, you're not alone. Laws are bills that have passed through a legislative branch (Congress) and have been signed by an executive branch (President) before they become law. Regulations are rules created by federal agencies like the ATF, Dept. of State, and Dept. of Commerce. All federal agencies report to the President and the regulations, or rules, they make explain how to comply with the law.

Each of these laws and regulations will be introduced and briefly discussed in Chapter 5 – Basic Firearm Compliance. In this chapter, only the requirements concerning the Federal Firearms Licensing system, and some necessary distinctions, will be discussed.

FFL licensing system

Some of the things implemented with the passing of the Gun Control Act of 1968 were the requirements of the federal firearm licensing system. There were licensing requirements before the GCA, but the GCA overturned much of the earlier law and made having a Federal Firearm License (FFL) a requirement for interstate commerce in firearms. This system established requirements for anyone "engaged on the business" of making or selling firearms.

Anyone with an FFL is called a Federal Firearm Licensee (also referred to as an "FFL"). I know that it's confusing but the term "FFL" is often used to refer to both the actual license and person/company that has the license.

Many of the requirements discussed in this book apply only to FFLs. For example, there are certain requirements for firearms markings (serial number, etc.) that only apply to firearms manufactured by an FFL. Contrary to popular belief, it is perfectly legal in certain circumstances for an individual to make their own firearms at home without markings. Once they intend to be engaged on the business of making or selling firearms, however, the requirement to have an FFL, and all of the associated requirements of FFLs, apply.

Required intent

A legitimate intent to be "engaged in the business of firearms" is necessary in order to get an FFL. The FFL application specifically asks whether you intend to make a profit from your business and if you intend to ONLY obtain personal firearms with your FFL. If you ONLY have a personal (non-business) purpose, then you won't get an FFL.

Categories of firearms

There are two main categories of firearms discussed in this book. The first category of firearms, which are controlled by the Gun Control Act of 1968, are "standard" firearms such as rifles, shotguns, pistols, and revolvers.

The second category of firearms, which are covered by the National Firearms Act of 1934 (NFA), have stricter controls. Some examples of these firearms are silencers, full-auto machine guns, short-barreled rifles, short-barreled shotguns, and more.

NOTE: I used the term silencers instead of suppressors. I know that it is popular to call them suppressors but the law and the ATF calls them silencers and you're here to learn what the law requires.

Of course, with the government, it's not always this simple. For example, silencers are also referenced in the GCA, but we still refer to them as an NFA firearm. And yes, even though a silencer doesn't shoot a bullet, it is still considered a firearm under the law. If these nuances are new to you, you should seriously consider learning more about ATF Compliance.

Although the GCA was passed 34 years after the NFA, the GCA is considered "Title I" of federal firearms laws and the NFA is considered "Title II."

These categories of firearms are generally referred to as GCA or Title I firearms or NFA or Title II firearms. As you'll see in the next chapter, there's no such thing as a "Class 3 firearm."

Chapter 3

FFL Types

In this chapter, we're going to cover:

- **Types of FFLs**
- **Classes of SOTs**
- **Which FFL is right for you**

FFLs/SOTs

There are currently 9 types of FFLs that can be broken down into four basic categories:

Collector – Not really covered by this book because this type of FFL is not for those "engaged in the business of firearms." This book will still help you but most of the information in this book is about modern firearms.

Dealer – These FFLs may purchase and sell guns as a business, and they may also operate as gunsmiths.

Manufacturer – There are two types of these FFLs: 1) manufacturers of firearms and ammunition, and 2) manufacturers of ammunition only. Firearm and ammunition manufacturers may, of course, manufacture firearms and ammunition and also act as a dealer and gunsmith. Ammunition manufacturers may only manufacture ammunition and may *NOT* act as a dealer or gunsmith.

Importer – These FFLs may import firearms and/or ammunition and also act as a dealer.

FFLs, by themselves, allow dealing, manufacturing, or importing of GCA / Title I firearms only. In order to deal, manufacture, or import NFA /Title II firearms, the FFL holder must also become a Special Occupational Taxpayer (SOT). Different classes of SOTs may engage in different activities.

Class 1 SOT – These SOTs may Import and deal NFA / Title II firearms

Class 2 SOT – These SOTs may manufacture and deal NFA / Title II firearms

Class 3 SOT – These SOTs may deal NFA / Title II firearms

Here's a good time to address some terminology that is very often misused in our industry. A Federal Firearm License (FFL) is something you have, while a Special Occupational Taxpayer (SOT) is something that you are. You don't get an "FFL and SOT." You get an FFL and become an SOT.

As I mentioned in the last chapter, "Class 3" is NOT a type of firearm. "Class 3" is a type of SOT an FFL holder is to deal in NFA firearms. An FFL holder can also be a "Class 1" or "Class 2" SOT, depending on whether they import and deal or manufacturer and deal NFA / Title II firearms

See the following table for a simplified breakdown of what each FFL/SOT combination allows. In the "FFL" column, you'll see each type of FFL. In the "purpose" column you'll see what that FFL, by itself, allows. In the "NFA /Title II" columns, you'll see what other activities the FFL holder may engage in if they are also a particular class of SOT. AP stands for Armor Piercing Ammunition and DD stands for Destructive Device.

		NFA/Title II (must be SOT)					
FFL	PURPOSE	DEALING	MANUFACTURING	IMPORTING	SOT CLASS	AP	DD
Type 01	Dealer or Gunsmith of Title I (GCA) Firearms	✓	✗	✗	3	✗	✗
Type 02	Pawnbroker dealing Title I (GCA) Firearms	✓	✗	✗	3	✗	✗
Type 03	Curio & Relic Collector	✗	✗	✗	-	✗	✗
Type 06	Manufacturer of Ammunition	✗	✗	✗	-	✗	✗
Type 07	Manufacturer/Dealer of Title I (GCA) Firearms	✓	✓	✗	2	✗	✗
Type 08	Importer/Dealer of Title I (GCA) Firearms	✓	✗	✓	1	✗	✗
Type 09	Dealer of Title I (GCA) Firearms	✓	✗	✗	3	✓	✓
Type 10	Manufacturer/Dealer of Title I (GCA) Firearms	✓	✓	✗	2	✓	✓
Type 11	Importer/Dealer of Title I (GCA) Firearms	✓	✗	✓	1	✓	✓

FFL and SOT

As a note, being an SOT is an option for all FFL holders but FFL types 3 and 6 and FFL Types 9, 10, and 11 are the only three FFLs that allow SOTs to work with Armor Piercing Ammunition and Destructive Devices. These three FFL holders are actually required to be SOTs - you can't just have these licenses by themselves.

For example, if you get a Type 7 FFL, you are allowed to manufacture and deal GCA / Title I firearms. If you also choose to become an SOT, then you may manufacture and deal

NFA / Title II firearms except for Armor Piercing Ammunition and Destructive Devices. If you also want to work with those, then you'll need to get a Type 10 FFL.

The Type 1 FFL allows you to be a dealer or gunsmith in firearms. This is the most common type of FFL. The Type 1 FFL is used by most local gun shops/gunsmiths. It allows the purchase of firearms for resale, and it allows the acceptance of firearms from individuals for gunsmithing and repair. If you are unsure which FFL to get, you likely should start here. This FFL will allow you to open up a gun store (storefront or home-based) and accept firearms for repair.

If you want to deal in NFA/Title II firearms, you're going to need to become a Class 3 SOT. This would allow you to deal in Silencers, Short Barreled Rifles, Short-Barreled Shotguns, Full-auto Machine Guns, and Any Other Weapons. It does not allow you to deal in Armor Piercing Ammunition or destructive devices.

The Type 2 FFL allows you to be a pawnbroker of firearms. There are certain allowances a Type 2 FFL has when returning firearms to residents of other states. Unless you specifically want to be a pawnbroker, this is not the FFL you are looking for. Just like the Type 1 FFL, you'll need to be a Class 3 SOT to work with NFA/Title II firearms, and you can't work with armor-piercing ammunition or destructive devices.

The Type 3 FFL is unique in that it is for collectors of firearms only. In effect, it is the only FFL that doesn't allow the holder to be engaged in the business of making or selling firearms or ammunition. A holder of this FFL may only collect "Curio and Relic" (C&R) firearms which are firearms that are at least 50 years old or which are on ATF's list of firearms that are collectible because of their historical connection. A Type 3 FFL holder may, however, have C&R firearms shipped directly to their licensed premises (most likely their home address) without having to go through another FFL for a transfer like they would for non-C&R firearms. With this type of FFL you can't be an SOT and you can't collect armor-piercing ammunition or destructive devices.

The Type 6 FFL is for manufacturers of ammunition ONLY - it does not allow you to work with firearms. This one should be self-explanatory. If you manufacture ammunition, you need this FFL. This includes components of ammunition, and not just completed cartridges. If you are also dealing in explosives (you make primers, for example), you are also going to need an explosives license. Just like with the Type 3 FFL, you can't be an SOT nor possess armor-piercing ammunition or destructive devices.

The Type 7 FFL is for Manufacturers of firearms. You can also deal firearms and manufacture ammunition with this license. Simply, if you want to manufacture firearms, you are going to need a Type 7 FFL. This seems simple enough, but there are a couple of tricky spots with this license. There are some activities that you may not think count as manufacturing. For example, assembling an AR-15 upper and lower together for resale is manufacturing.

If you become a Class 2 SOT this FFL will also allow you to manufacture most NFA firearms such as silencers, short-barreled rifles, short-barreled shotguns, machine guns, and "any other weapons." (Destructive Devices and Armor Piercing Ammo are not allowed). One of the biggest reasons I see for this FFL is the ability to manufacture machine guns and silencers. A dealer can only get a machine gun that was made after 1986 if they have a letter from a law enforcement agency requesting a demonstration of that particular firearm. A manufacturer, on the other hand, can make a machine gun whenever they want.

Once you start making NFA Firearms, you're likely going to need to register with the Directorate of Defense Trade Controls (DDTC) as part of ITAR (International Traffic in Arms Regulations. This is covered more in Chapter 20 - U.S. Dept. of State / Department of Commerce Compliance.

The Type 8 FFL is for importers of firearms. To import NFA/Title II firearms, you'll need to become a Class 1 SOT and you can't import Armor Piercing Ammunition or Destructive Devices. Here's a warning: there are marking requirements for importing firearms. You must mark your name and the city/state on the firearm - you can "adopt" the rest of the markings such as model, serial number, and caliber. This can get tricky if those other markings are not in English and are in a non-recognizable character (like Russian).

The Type 9 FFL is similar to the Type 1 FFL - you can be a dealer or gunsmith of firearms, and you need to be a Class 3 SOT in order to work with NFA firearms. The big difference with this type of FFL is it allows for dealing with Destructive Devices and Armor Piercing Ammunition. If you aren't going to deal with these, get a Type 1. If you are, get a Type 9.

The Type 10 FFL is similar to the Type 7 FFL - you can be a manufacturer and dealer of firearms, and you need to be a Class 2 SOT in order to make NFA/Title II firearms. This FFL allows the manufacture of Destructive Devices and Armor Piercing Ammunition. If you aren't going to make these, get a Type 7. If you are, get a Type 10.

The Type 11 FFL is similar to the Type 8 FFL - you can import firearms, and you need to be a Class 1 SOT in order to work with NFA/Title II firearms. This FFL allows the importation of Destructive Devices and Armor Piercing Ammunition. If you aren't going to import these, get a Type 8. If you are, get a Type 11.

FFL/SOT Cost

Your decision of which type of FFL to get is an important one. For example, if you get a Type 1 FFL now and later decide that you want to manufacture firearms, you are going to need to start over and get a Type 7 FFL. Now, you may think it is smarter to just get a Type 7 FFL in the first place, in case you decide to manufacture firearms at a later date. Well, it's not quite that simple. For example, as a firearm manufacturer, you might have to register with the U.S. State Department ($3,000 per year) if you manufacture items covered by ITAR, and you'll probably have to explain to the ATF your reasoning for getting a manufacturing FFL. "Because I might want to be a manufacturer someday" is probably not the best answer.

There's also a difference in the cost for the FFL and also the tax rate for becoming an SOT.

Although you save $50 on your application fee by being a manufacturer (it's only $150 for the first three years as a manufacturer while it's $200 for the first three years as a dealer), you'll pay $60 more than a dealer would at every FFL renewal ($150 for every three year renewal vs only $90 for each three year renewal). Also, the SOT tax rate for certain manufacturers can be as high as $1,000 per year, while dealers only pay $500 per year.

	FFL			SOT		
FFL	**Application Fee**	**Renewal Fee**	**Duration (years)**	**Tax-Rate (under $500k yearly sales)**	**Tax-Rate (over $500k yearly sales)**	**Duration (years)**
Type 1	$200	$90	3	$500	$500	1
Type 2	$200	$90	3	$500	$500	1
Type 3	$30	$30	3	n/a	n/a	1
Type 6	$30	$30	3	$500	$1000	1
Type 7	$150	$150	3	$500	$1000	1
Type 8	$150	$150	3	$500	$1000	1
Type 9	$3000	$3000	3	$500	$1000	1
Type 10	$3000	$3000	3	$500	$1000	1
Type 11	$3000	$3000	3	$500	$1000	1

As you can see, each FFL lasts for three years, and they vary in cost between the initial application fee which covers the first three years, and the renewal fee which covers each additional 3-year extension.

Both the Type 1 and Type 2 FFLs cost $200 for the first three years and $90 for each 3-year renewal. The Type 3 and 6 FFLs, neither of which can be used for being engaged in the business with firearms, are $30 for the initial fee and the renewals.

Both the Type 7 and 8 FFLs are $150 for the initial application and $150 for the renewals. Interestingly, well to me anyway, is that it is actually cheaper to get a manufacturer's license to make and sell guns than it is to just sell guns.

As mentioned above, although you save $50 on your application fee by being a manufacturer, you'll pay $60 more than a dealer would at every FFL renewal. So, years 4, 5, and 6 as a Type 1 dealer will only cost $290 while those same years as a manufacturer will cost $300. Also, as we'll cover next, the SOT tax rate for certain manufacturers can be as high as $1,000 per year while dealers only pay $500 per year.

The Type 9, 10, and 11 FFLs all jump up significantly in cost and are $3,000 for the initial cost and the renewal.

In addition to the license costs, we must also look at additional costs, such as SOT registration costs. We're going to have a brief look at SOT costs so that you can make a better decision about which type of FFL you want to get. A more in-depth conversation about Becoming an SOT is covered in the last section of this book.

Regardless of your yearly sales, the SOT registration cost for Type 1 and Type 2 FFLs is $500 and neither the Type 3 nor Type 6 FFLs can become an SOT.

For the remaining FFLs, if your yearly sales are under $500k, then the registration fee is $500. However, if you get a manufacturer's or importer's FFL, either the Type 7, 8, 10 or 11 FFLs, you must pay $1,000 if your annual sales are over $500k a year. If you're making that much money from your business, you shouldn't be too concerned with the extra $500 annually.

The Type 9 dealer's FFL stays at $500.

Which FFL is right for you?

So, which one should you get? Chances are, your choice is between a Type 1 dealer FFL or a Type 7 manufacturer FFL. These are the two most common types of FFLs.

However, only after you determine exactly what you want to do with your license can you decide which is the proper FFL to get. And, if you're wondering, YES you can have multiple FFLs and I often encourage it.

Section Notes

Chapter 1 - How to Use This book

- This book has 8 sections.
- You should work from beginning to end
- You can come back and review whenever you want

Chapter 2 - Background

Laws, regulations, and rules must ALL be followed

Main laws are:

- Gun Control Act of 1968 (GCA)
- National Firearms Act of 1934 (NFA)
- Arms Export Control Act (AECA)

Main Regulations are:

- ATF Firearm Regulations
- International Traffic in Arms Regulations (ITAR)
- Export Administration Regulations (EAR)

Two main categories of firearms:

- GCA Firearms (Standard Firearms - Rifles, Shotguns, etc.)

- NFA Firearms (Higher Restrictions - Silencers, Machine Guns, etc.)

Chapter 3 - FFL Types

There are currently 9 types of FFLs that can be broken down into four categories:

- Collector – Not covered by this guide because this type of FFL is not for those "engaged in the business of firearms."
- Dealer – These FFLs may purchase and sell guns as a business and they may also operate as gunsmiths.
- Manufacturer – There are two types of these FFLs: manufacturers of firearms and ammunition and manufacturers of ammunition only. Firearm and ammunition manufacturers may, of book, manufacture firearms and ammunition and also act a dealer. Ammunition only manufacturers may only manufacture ammunition and may *NOT* act as a dealer.
- Importer – These FFLs may import firearms and/or ammunition and also act as a dealer.

There are currently (C) 3 classes of SOT and each may engage in different activities:

- A Class 1 SOT may Import and deal NFA / Title II firearms
- A Class 2 SOT may manufacture and deal NFA / Title II firearms
- A Class 3 SOT may deal NFA / Title II firearms

INDIVIDUAL REQUIREMENTS

There are two sets of requirements for getting an FFL: Individual Requirements which apply to you as a person and Business Requirements which apply to your business or entity.

This section explores the first, Individual Requirements, and will cover what a "responsible person" is and how they (you) must be connected to the FFL and also a class of people called "prohibited persons" which may NOT be associated with your license.

Chapter 4

Responsible Persons

In this chapter, we're going to cover:

- **The definition of a Responsible Person**
- **Who is a Responsible Person for your FFL**
- **Requirements for Responsible Persons**

Responsible Person Definition

Every applicant for an FFL must designate at least one "responsible person" (RP) for the business. According to the ATF, "'responsible persons" are any individual possessing, directly or indirectly, the power to direct or cause the direction of the management and policies of the [business]." In plain language, a "responsible person" is anyone who can make decisions for and control firearms-related activity.

What does that mean? Well, the owner of a business is clearly an RP and their store manager might also be an RP. RPs are not necessarily the actual FFL-holders. The business has the FFL and the RPs are listed on the business's FFL. Only in the case of a sole-proprietorship would the business and the RP be the same person. Various business forms are discussed in Chapter 7 – Business Form.

Who is an RP for Your FFL?

It is important to note that the decision of who is an RP on a license is not about whether the person *wants to be* "on the FFL."

Instead, it's about their role in your business. If they meet the definition of an RP, they must be listed on the FFL.

This is an important distinction. I've heard many people say that they didn't want to be on the license so they never listed themselves as an RP. If the person can manage or control firearm compliance decisions, then they already meet the definition of an RP. If that RP isn't listed on the FFL, then the ATF won't be happy.

You should have more than one RP on your FFL. This is because if you are the only RP and something happens to you, then your survivors are going to have a difficult time continuing business operations. Even though someone else may be part owner of your business or they may inherit the business completely, if they aren't on the FFL as an RP, then there will be a period of time which the FFL will not have any RPs and may cause significant issues with the ATF.

Proper determination and listing of RPs is important to the ATF. First, the ATF can't talk to a business or necessarily hold a business accountable – they want a person in charge. Second, the ATF wants the opportunity to approve anyone in control of major decisions of an FFL. A part-time store employee does not need to be thoroughly vetted and approved by the ATF because they will be working under the supervision and direction of someone who has been vetted and approved, an RP.

If someone should be listed as an RP on the FFL and they are not, the ATF often views this as "hidden ownership or control" and can be a serious problem.

As I'll discuss later, I recommend applying for an FFL with only one RP listed on the application (if accurate and possible) and then adding additional RPs after you get the license. This technique will not risk your application being delayed because of multiple background checks and you can easily submit and add RPs later without the need to wait for formal approval.

Requirements for RPs

Each "responsible person" must submit fingerprints and photos to the ATF as part of the application/being added as an RP process. If you currently already have fingerprints and a photo on file because you are/were an RP on another FFL, then you can simply attach a note to your application asking the ATF to use the information that they already have on file.

Also, "responsible persons" must not be "prohibited persons" We're going to discuss what those are in the next chapter.

Chapter 5

Prohibited Persons

In this chapter, we're going to cover:

- **Restrictions on Prohibited Persons**
- **The definition of Prohibited Persons**
- **What items may not be possessed by Prohibited Persons**

Prohibited Person Definitions

"Prohibited persons" may not possess firearms nor ammunition. However, the law doesn't just apply to Prohibited Persons - it also applies to everyone else. It's unlawful for anyone to knowingly give a prohibited person firearms or ammunition. This means that you can't sell/rent/give a firearm or ammunition to a "prohibited person", you can't employ a "prohibited person," nor can you be a "prohibited person" yourself.

Those restrictions may seem straight-forward, but there are unique definitions and exceptions that apply. These details should be understood so that you know exactly who is a prohibited person and precisely what they are prohibited from possessing.

First, let's explore what is prohibited. It's important to understand, at a base-level, what counts as a firearm and ammunition under federal law.

Firearms/Ammunition

The basic definition of a firearm is: "any weapon (including a starter gun) which will or is designed to or may readily be converted to expel a projectile by the action of an explosive."

In simpler terms, this means that if a projectile (bullet) is shot out of an object because of an explosion (gun powder), then the object is a firearm.

It is not just the complete gun that counts as a firearm – the frame or receiver (or any object that can be readily converted into a frame or receiver) is also considered to be a firearm even though it can't fire a projectile by itself. Be careful here – this means that certain parts of a gun are treated as if they were complete firearms / guns.

It also means that objects that aren't fully completed yet can also be considered frames or receivers, and therefore firearms, if the ATF says that the object can be "readily converted" into a frame or receiver. More on these definitions can be found in our ATF Compliance book.

Also, silencers and "destructive devices" (grenades, explosive projectiles, etc.) are included in the federal definition of a firearm. These additional parts of the definition aren't worth discussing in this chapter, however, because if you are not permitted to possess a shotgun, you clearly aren't allowed to posses silencers and grenades.

There are some exceptions to the federal definition of firearms. For example, "antique firearms" are not considered to be firearms under federal law. Antique firearms are firearms that were made before 1899 for which ammunition is not readily available. The ammunition for these firearms can exist, it just can't be ammo commonly available. Antique firearms are also firearms that don't fire conventional ammunition cartridges - such as muzzleloaders. This means that a muzzle loader is considered an antique firearm, and therefore exempt from the federal definition of a firearm even if it was manufactured this morning.

Also exempt from the definition of a firearm are air guns. Remember, a firearm requires an explosion. No explosion = no firearm. Don't forget, this is the federal definition we're talking about. Some states, like New Jersey, define air rifles, such as pellet guns, as firearms.

The definition for ammunition is tricky. It includes a complete round/cartridge of ammunition and it also includes every component of ammunition. This means that cartridge cases, bullets (which are just the projectile), gunpowder, and primers are all considered to be ammunition by themselves. Therefore a prohibited person isn't allowed to posses even an empty cartridge case/piece of brass and you're not allowed to knowingly give a prohibited person that piece of brass.

Now we know what prohibit persons can't possess, next we need to figure out what a prohibited person is.

Who is a Prohibited Person?

The definition of who is a "prohibited person" includes many categories of people – they are included below. Some of the categories, like "felons," are simple. If someone is a felon, then they are prohibited from possessing firearms or ammunition. Other categories, however, aren't so clear and have specific details which are included below.

A "prohibited person" is anyone who:

- is a felon,
- has been convicted of any crime punishable by more than a year in prison (whether or not they were ever sentenced to or served a day in prison),
- is under indictment for any crime punishable by more than year in prison,
- is a fugitive,
- is an unlawful user of any controlled substance,
- has been adjudicated as a mental defective,
- has been committed to a mental institution,
- is an illegal alien,
- has a dishonorable discharge from the military,
- has renounced their U.S. citizenship,
- is the subject of a restraining order restraining the person from harassing, stalking, or threatening an intimate partner or the child of an intimate partner, or
- who has been convicted of a misdemeanor crime of domestic violence.

Domestic Violence / Restraining Orders

Most of the questions I receive about firearm possession by prohibited persons concern restraining orders or domestic violence charges. Unfortunately, some people have restraining orders against them even though they've never done anything wrong. If the restraining order is to prevent the harassment, stalking, or threatening of an intimate partner or their child, then the subject of the restraining order is a prohibited person and may not possess firearms while the restraining order is in effect.

It is important to note that an "intimate partner" does not need to be from a long-term relationship. Also, if there has been any conviction based on domestic violence, then the convicted person may not posses firearms. To see a detailed definition of what is considered a misdemeanor crime of domestic violence, and exceptions to the prohibition, see the ATF's guide on the topic: https://www.atf.gov/file/58786/download

Felons / Misdemeanors Punishable by Over a Year in Prison

Generally, crimes punishable by over a year in prison are felonies. We already know that all felons are prohibited persons. However, according to federal law, people that are convicted of misdemeanors that can be punished by over a year in prison even if the person is not actually sentenced to over a year in prison, are prohibited persons too.

There are some state-level misdemeanors that can have a punishment over a year in prison – especially repeat offenses. This can be tricky. For example, if a person has been convicted of a misdemeanor that has a listed punishment of 1 – 14 months in prison and the person's sentence didn't include any jail time, then they are still a prohibited person because they were convicted of a crime that was punishable (whether or not they received the punishment) by over a year in prison. For example, on a third DUI offense in the state of New York, the punishment can be for over a year even though it is still just a misdemeanor.

There's also an inconsistency here. Even though the law says misdemeanors of over a year in prison, the Form 4473, which is used for transfers of firearms to customers, has instructions on it which say that this provision doesn't include state misdemeanor crimes punishable by less than 2 years in prison. The takeaway here? Be careful when it comes to misdemeanors punishable by over a year in prison.

Unlawful Users of a Controlled Substance

With the recent legalization/de-criminalization of marijuana in some states, the use of a controlled substance part of the prohibited person definition is going to become a bigger issue. Just because your state may allow you to smoke marijuana, the federal government doesn't (yet).

Be careful.

Section Notes

Chapter 4 - Responsible Persons

- Every FFL must have at least 1 RP
- Someone is an RP by their role in the company, not their choice to be "on the FFL"
- RP's can't be prohibited persons

Chapter 5 - Prohibited Persons

- Prohibited Persons can't possess firearms or ammunition
- **You** can't knowingly allow a Prohibited Person to possess firearms or ammunition
- Be careful - some people may not even know that they're a Prohibited Person
- A "prohibited person" is anyone who:
  - *is a felon,*
  - *has been convicted of any crime punishable by more than a year in prison (whether or not they were ever sentenced to or served a day in prison),*
  - *is under indictment for any crime punishable by more than year in prison,*

- *is a fugitive,*
- *is an unlawful user of any controlled substance,*
- *has been adjudicated as a mental defective,*
- *has been committed to a mental institution,*
- *is an illegal alien,*
- *has a dishonorable discharge from the military,*
- *has renounced their U.S. citizenship,*
- *is the subject of a restraining order restraining the person from harassing, stalking, or threatening an intimate partner or the child of an intimate partner, or*
- *who has been convicted of a misdemeanor crime of domestic violence.*

BUSINESS/ENTITY REQUIREMENTS

The second set of requirements, Business/Entity Requirements, don't necessarily apply to you as a person – they are things that apply to your business.

Business requirements covered in this section include your business intent, the form of your business, and other details like location (the most important), hours of operation, and state-specific requirements.

Chapter 6

Business Intent

In this chapter, we're going to cover:

- **The "intent" requirement**
- **Intent to "Engage in the Business"**

If you intend to "engage in the business" of making or selling firearms, then you must have an FFL. Likewise, in order to obtain an FFL, you must have the intent to "engage in the business" of making or selling firearms.

Kinda' nice how that works out, eh?

Have the intent? Then get an FFL.

Want an FFL? Then have the intent.

What you intend to do with your FFL is so important, the word "intend" appears 5 times on the FFL application:

Box 9: Describe Specific Activity Applicant is Engaged in, or *Intends* to Engage in, Which Requires a Federal Firearms License.

Box 10: Do You *Intend* to Engage in Business as a Pawnbroker?

Box 18: Do You *Intend* To Make a Profit from Your Business?

Box 18a: Do You *Intend* To Sell Firearms Only at Gun Shows?

Box 19: Do You *Intend* to Use Your License Only to Acquire Personal Firearms?

Here's an important distinction: "Intend" is not the same as did/do/will do.

For example, a non-FFL can make their own firearms and they can even sell their own firearms. However, if they make the firearm with the intent to sell it, then they'll need an FFL.

I usually explain this distinction like this: With some limitations, you can make yourself your own bolt-action rifle without an FFL, you can bring the rifle to the range and have someone there admire it, and you can even sell it to them. However, what you can't do is agree to make them another rifle just like it for sale without an FFL. This is because you had no intent when you made the first rifle but you clearly would have the intent for the second rifle.

Be sure that you are aware of your intent now and only proceed with your application if your true and actual intent is to be engaged in the business of firearms. **Lying on this form is a serious violation!**

Note above that the question about your intent to acquire personal firearms does NOT prohibit you from using your FFL for personal firearms. Instead, you're only prohibited from using it ONLY to acquire personal firearms.

Once you've got a business intent, you need to form your business.

Chapter 7

Business Form

In this chapter, we're going to cover:

- **Establishing Your Business**
- **Choices of Business Form**
- **Business Considerations**
- **Business Types**

Establishing Your Business

Now that we've established your business intent, it's time to establish your business. You can run your business as a Sole Proprietor, as a company (LLC), as a partnership, or as a corporation (C-corp or S-corp).

Please consider forming a company or corporation instead of running your business as a sole proprietor. Being a sole proprietor is simpler up-front and it can have a benefit when you go out of business but I think it opens you up to too much liability and it may be more difficult to establish your business intent should it ever come into question.

Your business will be the applicant for the FFL. If your are a sole proprietor, this will be your name. If you establish a business entity, this will be in the business's name. In the next chapter, we'll discuss locations for your business. If you decide to run the business and FFL out of your home, you can obtain an off-site mailbox (such as a P.O. Box or UPS Store mailbox) as your mailing address for correspondence.

Firearms should only be delivered to your actual business/FFL location except in rare circumstances. It is perfectly legal for an FFL to have firearms shipped wherever they choose. However, you should keep this to a minimum. It is very easy to lose track of where firearms are being shipped, especially with back-orders or delayed shipments, and it can be difficult to ensure that someone who shouldn't receive and open the package doesn't end up in possession of the firearm. Also, a distributor might keep the alternate address in their system and accidentally ship future firearms there.

Business Considerations

Name

You need to give your Business a Name.

Technically, a business is a US-person. It is one of the few times that a male can "give life" to something (trusts are another example). Along with this privilege is the ability to give it a name! Choose your name carefully – it will be on your FFL! Your business name will also need to include your business type, for example, Smith Enterprises and More, LLC.

It does not mean, however, that the name you choose for the business is the name that you have to go by on a day-to-day basis. If you are going to be operating under another name, you will need to register the other name that you are doing business as. This is called a "DBA" which stands for "doing business as" (go figure). An example would be Smith Enterprises and More, LLC d/b/a Smitty's Guns. Your business will be recognized as (and pay taxes as) Smith Enterprises and More, LLC but you can have Smitty's Guns on your signage and business cards. If you go this route, your FFL will be issued to "Smith Enterprises and More, LLC d/b/a Smitty's Guns."

There is also a section on your FFL for "trade name." A trade name is a name that you can use for transfers and for marking firearms you manufacture as an FFL. For example, if your business name is Smith Enterprises and More, LLC, you can list "Smith Enterprises" as a trade name on your license. By doing this, you can list "Smith Enterprises" on your firearms and avoid having to list the "and More."

Registration

You will need to register your business in whichever state it is formed and located. It is not typically required that your business is registered/formed in your state of residence or even where you'll be conducting business. For example, there are many benefits to forming your business in another state such as Delaware and then registering your out-of-state business in the state where you expect to conduct business.

I like to register businesses in Delaware through a company called Harvard Business Services. They are FFL-friendly and can help by being your registered agent in Delaware and can even help you with your local state registration. I've included a link to them in the resources for the book at the URL/QR Code from the Introduction Section.

Taxes

Your choice of business form is an important one – this book does not replace actual legal advice nor tax guidance from an accountant. Please seek your own counsel when making this decision.

The good news about running a business is the tax-benefits. Yes, there are tax burdens too (these come with making money) – but if you work with a knowledgeable accountant, you can reap some great benefits! For example, if you want to produce YouTube videos for promotion for your business, you might be able to write-off your video production equipment (cameras, lights, tripods, video editing software, etc.) as well as business-property that you use in your videos for your business.

For example, if you upload a video of you shooting a machine-gun for promotion there's a good chance that your ammunition used in the video is a business expense! For my books on long range shooting, the Long Range Shooting Handbook and Advanced Long Range Shooting, I purchased some business equipment and tools (yes, guns, scopes, ammo, and gear CAN be tools) that I used for writing the books and for promoting them. I use it only for a business purpose, but there's no rule that says I can't enjoy the business-use of a certain tool that I might not have otherwise purchased.

Business Types

LLC

Usually, the best company form for an FFL is the Limited liability Company (LLC). Unfortunately, laws vary from state to state on how to form your own company and you'll need to seek out your own tax information or legal counsel to establish your own LLC.

If you'd like to use legal support to help you form your LLC, I recommend using RocketLawyer. Now, even though, they have an awesome name, we're not the same company. We do have a relationship with them though and they support FFLs. There's a link to them in the extra resources webpage a the URL/QR code in the Introduction Section.

Corporation

Corporations, like LLC's, can also afford you liability protection but they are a bit more difficult to establish and operate and depending on your state's laws and your unique corporation form, they can also involve more complicated and expensive tax considerations.

If you'd like to use legal support to help you form your corporation, use RocketLawyer.

Only attempt to do this on your own if you know what you are doing – improperly setting up your corporation or failing to file the documents properly with your state's Secretary of State could lead to troubles obtaining and keeping your FFL.

Start your corporation with RocketLawyer.com

S-Corporation

S-Corporations, like LLCs, are treated as "pass-through" entities where the tax burden passes through the corporation and to you as the owner. This can save "double taxation" problems but it can also set you up for a large personal tax obligation even without money ever passing from the LLC or S-Corporation to you. C-Corporations are subject to business tax first and then personal tax later once money is paid from the C-corporation to you.

EIN

If you form a business entity, you must obtain a federal Employer Identification Number (EIN). Your EIN is how your business will be identified by the ATF.

If you also become an SOT, your NFA transfers will be to and from your business entity as recognized by your EIN. This can help you if you have more than one FFL – transfers of NFA items among your FFLs under the same EIN do not require the normal ATF approval process for NFA transfers because it is the same entity in ATF's eyes. Be careful if you're planning on having multiple locations. The proper planning now can save you heartache later.

If this may be a potential issue for you, I suggest you finish this book without applying for an FFL (yet) so that you can learn about becoming an SOT before coming back to this chapter and making decisions about your business form.

If you use a sole proprietorship, you can use your Social Security Number (SSN) instead of an EIN but I recommend that you obtain an EIN anyway.

To get an EIN, go to the IRS's website at IRS.gov, search for creating/registering a new EIN and follow the process.

Chapter 8

Location

In this chapter, we're going to cover:

- **Business Location Requirements**
- **Differences Between Store-Front and Home-Based FFLs**
- **Special Considerations for Manufacturing**

"Location is Everything." That's not just what your real-estate agent tells you, it's what your firearm lawyer would tell you, too! Theres a chance that this might be the most complicated/involved section of this entire process. This chapter is so important because you may meet all of the other requirements for obtaining your FFL and if you are in the wrong location, you're aren't going to get it.

Local zoning ordinances will dictate whether your location is proper. As part of the initial inspection process by ATF (discussed in the Initial ATF Inspection section), the Industry Operations Investigator (IOI) will look into your location's zoning ordinances and confirm that your location is appropriate for your business. This hurdle may be significant for home-based FFLs and manufacturer FFLs.

Previously, the ATF would check with your local zoning office to confirm that you intend to operate in a proper location. However, lately the ATF has been requiring applicants to go the zoning office in advance and obtain written permission. In some instances this is merely a letter from the zoning office confirming that you're "good to go." However, sometimes a formal Use and Occupancy Permit may be required.

I've been told by ATF that this change is for two reasons. First, they'd rather not waste anybody's time if there's a zoning problem. Second, the Industry Operations Investigator (IOI) who is conducting your initial inspection doesn't want to sit in your local zoning office all day waiting to check on your location – they used to get expedited but lately zoning offices are making them "take a number" and wait like everyone else.

Retail Store-front

If you have a retail store-front zoned for commercial activity and you are obtaining a dealer or pawnbroker FFL, then you will likely not run into an issue obtaining your FFL. If you have an issue it will most likely be with a landlord who doesn't want a gun store in their building. Unfortunately, the landlord is able to determine which businesses they want in their buildings and you may be stuck finding an alternate location. If you are renting, the landlord's information must be included on your FFL application and the ATF will contact the landlord as part of your application process.

If at all possible you should ensure that your retail location is not near a school. Although it is unlikely to find a retail location within 1000 feet of a school, if your location is within that zone then firearms may only leave your store after they have been unloaded and locked in a case. More information on school-zones is discussed in the home-based business section below.

Home-based Business

Many of you are using this guide to get your FFL out of your home. Years ago, the ATF cracked-down on "kitchen-table" FFLs – those who ran their business out of their home. Currently, this is not the case and the number of FFLs based out of licensee's homes has been steadily increasing. Let me make this clear, you are PERFECTLY ABLE to get an FFL out of your home as long as you truly have the intent to be engaged in the business of firearms and your local zoning regulations allow your home-based business.

The first step is to go to your local zoning commission's website and searching for the zoning regulations for your neighborhood. You may find that it is perfectly legal for you to run a home-based business as long as you aren't conducting manufacturing activity (discussed below) or you won't have heavy customer traffic to your home. After all, you probably wouldn't like it if one of your neighbors had regular business-level traffic in front of their home.

The best possible scenario for a home-based FFL is a business intent that doesn't involve regular customers coming to your home. For example, I have helped people get their FFLs at home when they needed/used their FFL for non-retail business: gun writers, firearm reviewers (blogs/youtube videos), manufacturer's reps/sales staff, and professional shooters. Of book, you may still be able to sell firearms as long as you do not have a steady flow of strangers coming to your home to purchase firearms. For example, some home-based FFLs sell retail firearms only to those they know and certain VIP/special-case scenarios. It is not unreasonable to picture a home-based FFL who sells high-end/unique firearms to individuals/clients who expect discretion that they can not find in a neighborhood gun store.

It is VERY important that you have a legitimate intent to run a firearms business and not try to use your FFL only to collect personal firearms. As discussed in previous chapters, the intent is what matters. You may make an honest effort to run a business and end up not making a business profit. This is not a problem as long as you can honestly say that you are trying to run a business and have not yet been successful.

If your zoning rules do not allow a home-based business, you may have some work ahead of you. There are instances where your activity will rise to the level of requiring an FFL, even though you may not actually be "running a business" out of your home. You may need to contact your zoning commission to explain to them that your business activity is enough to be treated as a business for FFL purposes even though it may not rise to the level of a business that your zoning commission is trying to prevent. As an example, someone who reviews firearms online is likely making money from their reviews through advertising on their website or youtube.com. They are engaged in the business of firearms enough to require an FFL for receiving shipment of, and using, firearms for a business purpose. However, this is an activity that your local zoning commission may not have an issue with.

If your zoning commission refuses to work with you, you may need to find an off-site location where you can have your FFL. For example, local gun shops or other businesses have been known to allow the rental of a few square feet of their facility for your FFL. You can receive and store firearms there and also list your home later as an off-site storage location. Your home can be used to store the firearms for your FFL as long as you keep a log at the licensed location showing which firearms are not present and at the off-site location instead. Be warned that you may need to collect all of the firearms stored at your home and return them to the licensed location when an inspection of your FFL occurs.

> To whom it may concern:
>
> My intended business activity requires that I obtain a Federal Firearms License (FFL) at my home address, however, I will not be participating in business activity from my home that zoning rules intend to prevent.
>
> The Bureau of Alcohol, Tobacco, Firearms, and Explosives (ATF) regulates the firearms industry and issues FFLs. The ATF defines "engaged in the business" differently than the common use of the term. For example, even though I intend to have no public foot traffic to my home nor do I intend to have any retail operations, my business activity requires that I have an FFL because my company will make money related to firearms.
>
> No business activity will occur at my residence different from any other remote-work position. The business will just be me and a typical office desk - it will not involve any retail business on-site, public foot-traffic, nor will I be advertising my home as a place for customers to visit.
>
> I am writing to seek approval for my proposed business activity at this location. The ATF will likely contact you or your office in connection with my FFL application to confirm that my proposed business activity is, in fact, permitted at this location.
>
> If you have any questions, please do not hesitate to ask.

Manufacturing

In 3 separate instances (in two different states) I have personally obtained manufacturing FFLs in commercial office space not zoned for "manufacturing." This is because the ATF defines "manufacturing" differently than the common use of the term – which is what zoning departments and landlords typically use. For example, according to the ATF's use of the term, removing a rifle-length upper receiver from an AR-15 rifle and installing a short-barreled upper receiver, and thereby creating an NFA firearm, is "manufacturing." As you likely know, this can be completed without any tools – it is a matter of pushing out two pins, replacing uppers, pushing the pins back in, and properly registering (and marking, if needed) the newly-made NFA firearm, a Short Barreled Rifle (SBR). However, zoning departments and landlords typically define the term "manufacturing" to include machinery, tools, and a floor-full of metal chips and cutting oil.

In each of the instances, I obtained a manufacturing FFL in an area not zones for manufacturing activity, because I intended to occasionally "manufacture" an SBR from a standard AR-15 rifle and also because I intended to have firearms actually manufactured under a marking variance from the ATF which requires a manufacturers FFL even though the actual machining took place somewhere else.

In each case it required communication with the local zoning commissions and landlords. Typically this only involved phone calls and emails to each in order to get approval. However, in one case, it required me spending an afternoon in the zoning commission's office moving from department to department explaining why a manufacturing FFL was appropriate and required even though I wouldn't participate in the type of manufacturing they were worried about.

To aid you in your efforts, consider using the following language for your landlord and/or local zoning department if it applies to you:

> To whom it may concern:
>
> My intended business activity requires that I obtain a Federal Firearms License (FFL) for manufacturers (Type 07 FFL) even though no actual "manufacturing" activity will occur at this location.
>
> The Bureau of Alcohol, Tobacco, Firearms, and Explosives (ATF) regulates the firearms industry and issues FFLs. The ATF defines "manufacturing" very differently than the common use of the term. Typically, "manufacturing" includes machinery and tools to create a finished product out of raw material – this will not happen at this location. The ATF, however, defines "manufacturing" to include even occasional and minor assembly steps to an otherwise finished product. Also, if a firearm is completely manufactured (in the common sense of the term) at a different location by a different company (often in another state entirely) with my company's name on the firearm then a manufacturer's FFL is required by the ATF to tracking and record-keeping purposes.
>
> Again, no true manufacturing will occur at this location. No business activity will require actual manufacturing space nor require my business to be located within a district zoned for manufacturing. Instead, my business activity which requires this special manufacturer's FFL can be conducted without tools at a typical office desk.
>
> I am writing to seek approval for my proposed business activity at this location. The ATF will likely contact you or your office in connection with my FFL application to confirm that my proposed business activity is, in fact, permitted at this location.
>
> If you have any questions, please do not hesitate to ask.

Chapter 9

Hours of Operation

In this chapter, we're going to cover:

- **Hours of Operation**

You need REASONABLE hours of operation for your FFL. For example, a home-based FFL may only be open for a couple hours each day. However, on your application you must list legitimate hours of operation for your business. If you list only a couple of hours each Saturday, you may not be approved because the ATF may not believe that you are truly running a business. However, there is no requirement that your FFL-based business is a full-time venture for you.

The hours you list are important. These are the hours that the ATF should be able to expect to find you running your business. These are the hours that the ATF can come inspect you. They are not necessarily the only hours you can conduct business nor are they the hours that you must always be available – after all, you are allowed to take vacations! List good-faith hours that you intend to be available to run your business and if they change later, you can always amend your information with the ATF.

At a minimum, I recommend being available for about 10 hours a week. You don't necessarily need to spend this much time running your business, but any less than that and the ATF might be concerned that you don't really need an FFL.

Chapter 10

State-Specific Requirements

In this chapter, we're going to cover:

- **ATF Requirements**
- **State-Specific General Requirements**
- **State-Specific Licensing Requirements**

ATF Requirements

State-level laws matter to the ATF?!?! Yes!

Many think that the ATF only enforces federal laws and regulations. Those people are right, however, that doesn't mean that the ATF doesn't care about/know your state-level, and possibly county-level, laws. In fact, the ATF requires you to follow your state-level laws and they, even as a federal agency, will cite you with violations on an inspection (and perhaps worse) for failing to follow you state's laws. This is because there is a catch-all federal rule that says you must follow the ATF's rules AND all other laws. Therefore, you can get into trouble with the ATF for not following your state's rules because that would violate a federal catch-all regulation.

The state rules you need to be aware of and follow aren't limited only to firearms-related rules. In fact, there are many non-firearm-specific rules you must still follow. For example, you'll need to collect any required state, county, and/or city sales tax, you'll likely need to have your business registered with your state(s), you'll have to complete any necessary paperwork/business filings with the state, you'll need to follow the employment laws of your state (including worker's comp), and you'll need to follow your city/county zoning laws (as we discussed earlier). These requirements apply to all business activity – not just FFLs.

State-Specific General Requirements

Legal Advice Note: Although I am an attorney, I am not your attorney nor am I licensed in all of these states. Therefore, any information about state-level and/or county-level laws and regulations is NOT legal advice. If you are looking for state-specific legal advice, you MUST find and hire your own attorney licensed in your state.

Taxes

You've got to pay your taxes. Sorry for the bad news. The good news is that you may be able to enjoy some nice business write-offs. (This was discussed in Chapter 7 – Business Form) Work with your accountant to ensure that you are doing this properly!

Business Registration

As mentioned in Chapter 7 – Business Form, you must register your business where the business is formed and where you are conducting business – this can be two (or more) different states. If your business is formed in another state, you will likely registering your business in your home-state as a "foreign entity" (foreign to your state, not your country). The ATF will want to see your business registration during your initial inspection and before they issue you an FFL.

Business Filings

Many states require certain filings in addition to tax documents. You must research your own state's requirements. This is where a good accountant comes in handy!

Employment Requirements

I've seen many FFLs get jammed-up over employment issues. There are federal employment requirements too. For example, you can't employ prohibited persons (discussed in Chapter 5 – Prohibited Persons) and more topics will be discussed later in Chapter 19 – ATF Compliance.

If you hire employees, pay particularly close attention to worker's compensation requirements, insurance rules, and state environmental rules.

State-Specific and/or County-Specific Licensing Requirements

If you live in a state, or county, with extra firearms rules for FFLs (above and beyond the federal rules) you probably already know. Even if you know that you live in a state or county with extra requirements, there are likely requirements that you aren't aware of.

I had originally listed out the requirements, by-state, below, however, I quickly realized that this book would be giving out-dated information quickly because state and local requirements can change so often. Also, simply listing out the number of states, counties, and cities with requirements would likely be longer than this entire book.

Therefore, this book focuses on federal laws and rules and you MUST look into local requirements yourself.

Section Notes

Chapter 6 - Business Intent

- "Intent" required
- No requirement to sell a certain amount of money / make a certain number of sales
- Simply listing a firearm on gunbroker.com or charging for the occasional transfer can count

Chapter 7 - Business Form

- You must establish a business and pick a business location
- There are various business considerations:
  - The name of your business (vs. the trade name)
  - You must decide where to register your business
  - There are various tax considerations
- You have a choice among business types:
  - LLC - recommended
  - Corporation (C or S Corp)

- You'll need to establish an EIN for your business - this is how you'll be recognized by the ATF

Chapter 8 - Location

- This may be the toughest part of getting your FFL
- Proper zoning is imperative
- Home-based business are allowed by the ATF
- "Manufacturing" may not mean the same thing to the ATF as it does to your zoning department

Chapter 9 - Hours of Operation

- You need "reasonable" hours of operation
- This is when the ATF may inspect you

Chapter 10 - State Specific Requirements

- Some states have rules about the form of, and registration of, your business that you must look into and adhere to.

FFL APPLICATION

Finally – the section you've been waiting for: the actual FFL Application.

This section will walk you through the application itself but, hopefully, you've read the previous sections so that you know about all of the requirements and you've learned enough to help you make some decisions along the way.

Please follow the instructions in this section exactly as they are written.

Chapter 11

Application Process

In this chapter, we're going to cover:

- **FFL Application Process**

The application process itself is actually fairly simple. You will be sending one packet of paperwork to the ATF, one copy of your application to your local Chief Law Enforcement Officer (CLEO), and you will keep one copy for your records.

In the following chapters I'll walk you through how to fill out the application and what you need to include in your packet to the ATF and envelope to your CLEO.

Don't worry about each piece now – I'm including the information below to give you an idea of what we're going to cover. By the time you're done with this section, all forms will be complete and I'll provide you a simple checklist to use to make sure you're ready to go!

FFL Application Process:

- Complete FFL Application (Form 7, 5310.12)[1]
- Get 2×2″ Photograph for each "Responsible Person"
- Complete Fingerprint Cards (FD-258) for each "Responsible Person"
- Draft check (or pay by credit card on application) for dollar amount of your chosen FFL type

1. Available by following the URL/QR Code in the Introduction section.

- Send the above materials to the ATF
- Send one copy of FFL Application to your local Chief Law Enforcement Officer
- Wait for ATF to process application and schedule initial interview

Chapter 12

Complete FFL Application

In this chapter, we're going to cover:

- **Methods of filling out application**
- **Instructions for the application**
- **Sample application**

Methods to Fill Out Application

Your application for your FFL may be filled out in a few different ways:

1. Ordering a copy from the ATF, or
2. Downloading and printing a PDF of the application (on white paper)

Electronically: If you prefer to fill out the application electronically (before printing), you may:

Open the PDF of the application[1], fill it out on your computer screen, and then print it once complete (on white paper)

I have created a sample FFL Application for you to review and use to help you fill out your application. It is included at the end of this chapter.

By Hand: You may fill out a paper version of the application in BLACK INK by:

Starting with a printed application (either from the ATF or one that you printed yourself) and fill in each section by hand by following the instructions below.

---

1. Available by following the URL/QR Code in the Introduction section.

Instructions for the Application

Please see below for notes for each question on the application. I suggest you follow along with each number.

First, you are going to fill out the "ATF Copy" of the application. The "copy" information can be found at the bottoms of the application pages. "ATF Copy" is only the first four pages of the 12 page application.

If you pay by check, instead of credit card, you may ignore the "CLEO Copy" completely. This is because the "CLEO Copy" (pages 9-12 of the application) is identical to the "ATF Copy" except for having the credit card information section missing. With a check, there's no credit card information to protect and therefore a duplicate of the "ATF Copy" (either a second printing or a photocopied version) works just fine... and it reduces the chance for error of filling out two separate forms.

If you want an example of government inefficiency, look no further than the previous version of the form. It had four "copies" instead of the current two - there were two copies for the ATF (even though they long since have required only one), one CLEO copy, and the fourth was for your records.

Folks were welcome to complete "copy 4" if they liked, but I always insist that you make a photocopy or electronic scan of ANY document you send to the ATF anyway so you are going to have a copy of the original "ATF Copy" that you sent to the ATF for your files.

As a general rule, I don't like to leave spaces on forms blank – if you don't have relevant information for any particular section, please write "n/a."

STEP 1. Fill out "Part A" of the "ATF Copy" of your FFL application.

I've included notes for each application question below. Once you've followed the notes below for Part A, come back here to continue with Step 2.

STEP 2. Have EACH Responsible Person (RP) fill our their own copy of "Part B" of the "ATF Copy" (see notes below).

I've included notes for each application question below. Once you've followed the notes below for Part B, come back here to continue with Step 3.

STEP 3. If needed, transfer relevant information from both parts of the "ATF Copy" of the application to the "CLEO Copy."

STEP 4. Print out your application (if completed electronically).

If you filled out the application by hand, laugh at the computer-nerds who have one more step than you.

STEP 5. Initial each of the six boxes in #20, and sign #21 of "Part A"

STEP 6. Have EACH Responsible Person (RP) sign #40 of their "Part B," attach their photo, and print their full name under their photo.

As I mentioned in the notes below, you MUST be honest on this form. If you are in doubt of the accuracy of any of your answers, STOP and don't finish the form and don't submit it to the ATF. If you lie on this form and then submit it to the ATF, you can be in a world of trouble.

STEP 7. Make a copy (photocopy or scan) of the complete "ATF Copy" of your application.

This copy is for your records. You should start a file now to keep all documents and correspondence with the ATF – this will be the first document in that file.

NOTES for Each Question on the Application - PLEASE FOLLOW ALONG

PART A

Applicant's Business Activity is: Select the type of business entity you've decided to apply as. The most common options will be "Individual Owner," Corporation," and "LLC."

Licensee Name. If you are applying as an individual, you put your full name here (e.g. John J. Smith). If, however, you are using a business, you place the full business name here – be sure to include the LLC, Inc., or Corp. where appropriate! (e.g. Smith Enterprises, LLC).

Trade or Business Name. This is a name that you may want to use other than your official company name. For example, Smith Enterprises, LLC probably doesn't want that name on the firearms they manufacture. Instead, they like the name "SmithGuns." Therefore, they would include "SmithGuns in this section of the application. If the name isn't in Section 1 or this section, it can't be used as the FFL's name for ATF transactions. This is because the ATF wouldn't be able to trace a firearm marked "SmithGuns" unless they knew that it was a name used by Smith Enterprises, LLC.

Employer Identification Number (EIN). If you are applying as a business, you should already have an EIN. If you do not, go get one first and then come back and finish the application. You may obtain an EIN from the IRS HERE.

Name of County in Which Business is Located. Note that there is no "R" in the previous sentence. It is "county" and NOT "countRy."

Business/Activity Address. This is the address of the licensed premises – it is where the ATF expects to find you conducting your business. This can not be a P.O. Box. As we already covered, you may have an off-site storage location for firearms – do not include that address here.

Mailing Address. If you want mail delivered to another address, you may include that here. This address may be a P.O. Box.

Contact Numbers. Ensure that you include an area code with each number you provide. It is not necessary to have a fax number. If you list a number for a cell phone the you always have with you, you don't need to list a separate 24 hour emergency number. Also, your business phone and your cell phone may be the same number.

Describe Specific Activity Applicant is Engaged in, or Intends to Engage in, Which Requires a Federal Firearm License. Examples of suitable answers for this question include: "Firearm Dealer," "Firearm Manufacturer," "Gunsmith," or "Ammunition Manufacturer." Please list whatever is relevant to your situation. Your answer here should match the license type you select in Question 10.

Application is Made For a License Under 18 U.S.C. Chapter 44 as a: Select the license type you want. Refer back to the section on license types if you need help deciding which license type is right for you. At the bottom of the column, write in the dollar amount for the application fee based on your selection.

Method of Payment. Personally, I prefer to use a check because it is easier for me to track with paperwork but you may use whichever method of payment you like. If you choose to use a credit card, make sure all of the credit card information is filled out properly with the billing address for the credit card – not necessarily the licensed premisses address. You do not sign here unless you are using a credit card.

Hours of Operation. These are the hours during which ATF expects to be able to stop by and see you in person. This is a tricky spot on the application. You need to have some regular hours of operation during which the ATF knows that they can contact you! It is not necessary, however, that you are open full-time. There is no clear answer on how many hours is enough – just make sure you have some regular hours during which you can generally be found at the licensed premises if the ATF wants to come do an inspection or contact you. It is not a rule that you absolutely must be there for every minute of your business hours but you should try to usually be available – ATF won't be happy if they show up during your business hours and find an empty building. If the hours you selected aren't working for you after you get your FFL, you may amend your hours of operation (or most other information) by filling out and submitting an Application for an Amended Federal Firearms License (ATF Form 5300.38). On the this form, the ATF specifically asks that you keep at least one hour available during which you can be contacted by the ATF. If you aren't open to the public, you may try to put "available by appointment only" for most (all?) days.

Was the business obtained from someone else? Select the correct answer. The name of the previous business owner and FFL number only apply only if you obtained your business from someone else. The ATF is concerned with a a non-compliant dealer passing off the store and FFL into someone else's name.

Indicate Type of Business Premises: Select the appropriate answer based on your research earlier in this process.

Applicant's Premises Is: If you do not own the licensed premises, and you're not on a military base, you must select "leased/rented" and fill out the relevant information for the property owner. This is true even if you are using a space for free and aren't technically paying rent. The ATF isn't concerned with the amount of rent, they are concerned with contacting the property owner to ensure that the owner is aware, and approves of, an FFL on the property.

Do You Intend to Sell Firearms at Gun Shows and/or Conduct Internet Sales: Select accordingly. Even if you select "No" because that is your current intent, you can always change your intent later. However, if you have zoning issues and will only sell online and at gun shows, make sure you select "yes."

Do You Intend to Use Your License ONLY to Acquire Personal Firearms to Enhance Your Personal Collection? As mentioned above, you may not have an FFL with the *INTENT* to use it only for personal purposes. Therefore, you may only have an FFL if your honest answer to this question is "No." Again, this question is about your *INTENT* and not what actually ends up happening. For example, if the only gun acquired on your license is a personal firearm, you aren't breaking the law as long as you *INTEND*(and try) to find customers and sell firearms.

Name of Chief Law Enforcement Officer: If you are unsure whether this is your Chief of Police of Sheriff, you can always call and ask.

Address of CLEO: Enter the mailing address for the CLEO from #18 and be sure to enter the county in which they are located.

Applicant Certification: If you're filling out the form by hand, you can read and initial these now. If you're filling out the form on your computer, you can skip this for now and come back to it after you've printed the form.

Certification: Fill out your name in the "Print Applicant name" section and enter the date. If you're filling out the form by hand, you can also sign the form now. If you're filling out the form on your computer, you can skip the signature for now and come back to it after you've printed the form.

After completing box 21, return above and continue with Step 2.

PART B

License or Applicant Name: Enter the same information from #2 of Part A

Federal Firearms License Number: This section is ONLY for adding a Responsible Person to a current FFL

Name of Responsible Person: Enter the name of the RP filling out the form (you may not fill out this form for someone else)

Aliases. Include any aliases if they exist (this includes maiden names)

Position/Title. Enter the position or title you hold within the company (owner/manager/salesman/etc.)

Social Security Number. Enter the RP's SSN

Date of Birth. Enter the RP's date of birth.

Place of Birth. Enter the RP's place of birth.

Current Residence Address. Enter the current residence address of the RP (not of the business)

Telephone Number. Enter the RP's personal (not business) telephone number.

Email Address. Enter the RP's email address (business email is ok)

Previous Addresses. Enter every address for the past five years. Add an extra sheet if necessary. The extra sheet of information must list the following information at the top of the sheet: RP's Name and Social Security Number.

Sex. Self explanatory.

Height. Self explanatory.

Weight. Self explanatory.

Eye Color. Self explanatory.

Hair Color. Self explanatory.

Ethnicity. Self explanatory.

Race. Self explanatory.

Questions 20-25. If yes, list the FFL number(s) as needed and add an additional sheet with details. The extra sheet of information must list the following information at the top of the sheet: RP's Name and Social Security Number.

See above

See above

See above

See above

See above

If someone has been, or is, any of the things listed in Questions 26-34, then they can not be a Responsible Party on your FFL. Even more, they can't be in possession of firearms or ammunition!

As we covered earlier, a Responsible Person is someone who is on your FFL and who "possess[es], directly or indirectly, the power to direct or cause the direction of the management, policies, and practices of the [business] insofar as they pertain to firearms." Not having someone fill out Part B does not prevent them from being considered a Responsible Person. Instead, a person is a Responsible Person by virtue of their abilities and must be added to the FFL. I add this because I've had clients who were in charge of the company but didn't "want to be on the license so they couldn't get in trouble." They were already a Responsible Person because of their position – they were actually inviting trouble by not being listed as a Responsible Person on the license like there are supposed to be.

To make your application process easier, I recommend limiting the number of Responsible Persons you add at this time. This does NOT meant to hide or avoid listing an RP. If someone is clearly an RP, then they should be a part of the application. However, if your business is just starting and you;re not exactly sure who else will be an RP yet, you can add them after you get your license.

After you get your license, you can easily add as many Responsible Persons as you like by having them fill out Part B and sending it in with their photo and fingerprints and later from you, as the RP, asking them to be added as an RP to your license.

Any "yes" answers require an explanation on an attached sheet of paper. The extra sheet of information must list the following information at the top of the sheet: RP's Name and Social Security Number.

Questions 26-34. Answer these questions carefully and honestly! If you need help with these, go back and review the chapter on Responsible Persons.

See above

See above

See above

See above

See above

See above

See above

See above

Country of Citizenship. Select USA or "Other" and list the country. Nationals of the USA should select "USA"

See #26 above

See #26 above

Are you an alien who has been admitted to the United States under a non-immigrant visa? If you select "No" for #38a, then select "N/A" for #38b. This includes, among others, persons visiting the United States temporarily for business or pleasure, persons studying in the United States who maintain a residence abroad, and certain temporary foreign workers. The definition does NOT include permanent resident aliens nor does it apply to nonimmigrant aliens admitted to the United States pursuant to either the Visa Waiver Program or to regulations otherwise exempting them from visa requirements.

If you are an alien, record your US-Issued Alien or Admission Number. If you answered "No" to #38, then skip this step.

Certification. Each RP should fill out their name in the "Printed Name" section and enter the date. If you're filling out the form by hand, you can also sign the form now. If you're filling out the form on your computer, you can skip the signature for now and come back to it after you've printed the form.

After completing box 40, return above and continue with Step 3.

Sample Application

OMB No. 1140-0018

U.S. Department of Justice
Bureau of Alcohol, Tobacco, Firearms and Explosives

Application for Federal Firearms License

Part A

1. Applicant's Business/Activity is: ☐ Individual Owner *(Sole Proprietor)* ☐ Partnership ☐ Corporation ☑ LLC
☐ Collector *(which can be an individual/partnership/corporation or LLC)* ☐ Other *(specify)*

2. Licensee Name *(Enter name of Owner/Sole Proprietor OR Partnership (include name of each partner) OR Corporation Name OR LLC Name)*
Smithsonian Enterprises, LLC

3. Trade or Business Name(s), *if any*	4. Employer Identification Number *(EIN), if any (see definition #17)*	5. Name of County in which Business/Activity is Located
Smithsonian Shop	12-3456789	Henry

6. Business/Activity Address *(RFD or Street Number, City, State, and ZIP Code) (NOTE: This address CANNOT be a P.O. Box.)*	7. Mailing Address *(if different from address in item #6)*
123 Historical Ave, Nashville, TN 37011	P.O. Box 123, Nashville, TN 37011

8. Contact Numbers *(Include Area Code)*
Business/Activity Phone 615-867-5309 Fax Number N/A
Cell Phone 615-100-2000 Business Email Info@SmithsonianShop.com

9. Describe the specific activity applicant is engaged in or intends to engage in, which requires a Federal Firearms License *(sale of ammunition alone does not require a Federal Firearms License).*
firearms dealer

10. Application is made for a license under 18 U.S.C. Chapter 44 as a: *(Place an "X" in the appropriate box(es). Multiple license types may be selected- see instruction #8. Submit the fee noted next to the box(es) with the application. Licenses are issued for a 3-year period. See instruction #5 for payment information).*

Type	Description of License Type	Fee
01	Dealer in Firearms Other than Destructive Devices *(Includes: rifles, shotguns, pistols, revolvers, gunsmith activities, and National Firearms Act (NFA) weapons) (see instruction #10)*	$200 ☒
02	Pawnbroker in Firearms Other than Destructive Devices *(Includes: rifles, shotguns, pistols, revolvers, gunsmith activities, and National Firearms Act (NFA) weapons) (see instruction #10)*	$200 ☐
03	Collector of Curios and Relics *(NOTE: This is not a license to conduct business, see instruction #8)*	$30 ☐
06	Manufacturer of Ammunition for Firearms Other Than Ammunition for Destructive Devices or Armor Piercing Ammunition *(see instruction #11)*	$30 ☐
07	Manufacturer of Firearms Other than Destructive Devices *(see instruction #11)*	$150 ☐
08	Importer of Firearms Other than Destructive Devices or Ammunition for Firearms Other than Destructive Devices, or Ammunition Other than Armor Piercing Ammunition *(NOTE: Importer of handguns and rifles, see instruction #9)*	$150 ☐
09	Dealer in Destructive Devices *(see instruction #10)*	$3000 ☐
10	Manufacturer of Destructive Devices, Ammunition for Destructive Devices, or Armor Piercing Ammunition *(see instruction #11)*	$3000 ☐
11	Importer of Destructive Devices, Ammunition for Destructive Devices, or Armor Piercing Ammunition *(see instruction #9)*	$3000 ☐
	Total Fees	$ 200

11. Method of Payment *(Check one)*

☑ Check *(Enclosed)* ☐ Cashier's Check or Money Order *(Enclosed)* ☐ Visa ☐ Mastercard ☐ American Express ☐ Discover ☐ Diner's Club

Credit/Debit Card Number *(No dashes)*	Name as Printed on Your Credit/Debit Card	Expiration Date *(MM/YY)*
N/A	N/A	N/A

Credit/Debit Card Billing Address: Address: N/A
City: N/A State: N/A ZIP Code: N/A

Please complete to ensure payment is credited to the correct application:

I am paying the application fee for the following Person, Corporation, or Partnership:	**Total Application Fees:**
N/A	$ N/A

I authorize ATF to charge my Credit/Debit Card the above amount. Your credit/debit card will be charged the above stated amount upon receipt of your application and a charge from "ATF Licensing Fee" will be reflected on your credit/debit card statement. In the event a license is NOT issued, the above amount will be credited to the credit/debit card noted above.

N/A N/A
Signature of Cardholder Date

ATF Copy - Page 1

ATF Form 7(5310.12)/7CR(5310.16)
Revised October 2020

FFL Application Page 1

12. Hours of Operation and/or Availability of Business/Activity *(please provide at least one hour in which you can be contacted by ATF personnel)*

	Sun	Mon	Tues	Wed	Thu	Fri	Sat
Hour(s): Please indicate AM or PM	N/A	8:00a.m.-12p.m.	N/A	8:00a.m.-12p.m.	N/A	8:00a.m.-12p.m.	By Appointment

IF YOU ARE **ONLY** APPLYING FOR A TYPE 03 (COLLECTOR OF CURIOS AND RELICS) LICENSE, SKIP ITEMS 13-17 AND GO TO ITEM 18. FOR ALL OTHER LICENSE TYPES, CONTINUE WITH ITEM 13.

13. Was the business obtained from someone else? *(If "Yes," please provide the name of the previous business and their FFL Number)* ☐ Yes ☑ No

N/A
Name of Previous Business

N/A
Federal Firearms License Number

14. Indicate type of business premises

Zoned Residential:
- ☑ Single Family Dwelling
- ☐ Condominium/Apartment
- ☐ Hotel/Motel
- ☐ Public Housing

Zoned Commercial:
- ☐ Store Front
- ☐ Office
- ☐ Rod & Gun Club
- ☐ Military Installation *(see instruction #13-additional information required)*
- ☐ Other *(specify)*

15. Applicant's business premises is:

☐ Owned Premises
☐ Military Installation
☑ Rented/Leased Premises- provide name, telephone number, and address **of the property owner**:

Jim John
Name

789 Anytown Drive
Street Address

615-456-7777
Telephone Number *(with area code)*

Nashville, TN 37012
City, State, and ZIP Code

16. Do you intend to sell firearms at Gun Shows and/or conduct Internet sales? ☑ Yes ☐ No

17. Do you intend to use your license ONLY to acquire firearms to enhance your personal collection? ☐ Yes ☑ No

18. Name of Chief Law Enforcement Officer *(CLEO) (Please print the name of the CLEO to whom a copy of this application was provided. See instruction #4 and definition #1.)*

Sheriff Abe Lincoln

19. Address of CLEO *(Include Number, Street, City, County, State, and ZIP Code)*

456 Patriot Lane, Nashville, TN 37013

county: Henry

ATTENTION Chief Law Enforcement Officer (CLEO): This form provides notification of a person's intent to apply for a Federal Firearms License (FFL). It requires no action on your part. However, should you have information that may disqualify the person from obtaining a Federal Firearms License, please contact the Federal Firearms Licensing Center toll free at 1-866-662-2750. Issuance of an FFL in no way guarantees the business or activity is not in violation of State and/or local law.

20. **Applicant Certification** ***(Please read AND INITIAL each box)***

☒ a. The business/activity to be conducted under the Federal Firearms License is not prohibited by State or local law at the premises shown in item 6. This includes compliance with zoning ordinances. ***(Please contact your local zoning department PRIOR TO submitting application)***

☒ b. Within 30 days after the application is approved, the business/activity will comply with the requirements of State and local law applicable to the conduct of the business/activity.

☒ c. Business/activity will not be conducted under the license until the requirements of State and local law applicable to the business/activity have been met.

☒ d. A completed copy of this application has been sent *(mailed or delivered)* to the Chief Law Enforcement Officer (CLEO) of the locality in which the premises listed in item 6 is located *(see instruction #4 and definition #1)*.

☒ e. As required by 18 U.S.C. 923 (d)(1)(G), I certify that secure gun storage or safety devices will be available at any place in which firearms are sold under this Federal Firearms License to persons who are not licensees. *(See definition #4) (If applying for a Type 03, Collector of Curios and Relics License ONLY, write "N/A" instead of initialing this certification box.)*

☒ f. Part B of this application has been completed and will be submitted for EACH responsible person (RP) *(See definition #3)*

21. Certification: Under the penalties imposed by 18 U.S.C. 924, I declare that I have examined this application in its entirety and the documents submitted in support thereof and to the best of my knowledge and belief, they are true, correct, and complete. This signature, when presented by a duly authorized representative of the U.S. Department of Justice, will constitute consent and authority for the appropriate U.S. Department of Justice representative to examine and obtain copies and abstracts of records and to receive statements and information regarding the background of the applicant. Specifically, I hereby authorize the release of the following data or records to ATF: Military information/records, medical information/records, police and criminal records. This certification must be signed by a Responsible Person *(see instruction #2 and definition #3)*.

Jim John Smith
Print Applicant Name *(First, Middle, Last)*

Applicant Signature

11/01/2020
Date

Check Application Status (For ATF Use Only) ☐ Approved ☐ Abandoned ☐ Withdrawn ☐ Denied Reason for Denial:

Signature of Licensing Official: Date:

ATF Copy - Page 2

ATF Form 7(5310.12)/7CR(5310.16)
Revised October 2020

FFL Application Page 2

Part B - Responsible Person Questionnaire

1. **EACH RESPONSIBLE PERSON MUST COMPLETE AND SIGN A SEPARATE QUESTIONNAIRE/ATF Form 7/7CR Part B.** In the future, if you need to add an additional Responsible Person *(RP)* to your FFL, the RP being added may complete this Part B-Responsible Person Questionnaire. If adding a RP to an existing license, be sure to include a signed written request from an existing RP on the license, giving permission to add the new Reponsible Person ***(see instruction #7)***.
2. Issuance of your license or addition as a Responsible Person will be delayed if Part B is incomplete or otherwise improperly prepared.
3. IMPORTANT! All new responsible persons must submit a properly prepared FD-258 *(Fingerprint Card)* with this questionnaire. The fingerprints must be clear for accurate classification and taken by someone properly equipped to take them. The FD-258 should include "WVATF1100 ATF-FFLC, MARTINSBURG, WV" in the ORI block to facilitate processing of fingerprints.
4. LIST any given, married, and maiden names in Item 4, e.g., "Mary Alice (Smith) Jones," not "Mrs. John Jones." (If additional space is needed, attach a separate sheet. See instruction #1)

1. License or Applicant Name *(From block 2 of Part A)* Smithsonian Enterprises, LLC	2. Federal Firearms License Number *(If being added to an existing FFL)* N/A

3. Name of Responsible Person *(Last, First, Middle)* Jim John Smith	4. Aliases *(Include given, married, maiden names)* N/A	5. Position/Title Owner

6. Social Security Number 123-45-6789	7. Date of Birth *(MM/DD/YYYY)* 10/10/1979	8. Place of Birth *(City & State OR foreign country)* Phoenix, AZ

9. Current Residence Address 123 Historical Ave, Nashville, TN 37011	10. Telephone Number *(Personal Contact # with Area Code)* 615-100-2000 11. E-mail Address JJsTaterSalad@Gmail.com

12. Previous Address(es) - Please provide every address you have had in the last five years and dates which you lived at the address(es) *(If additional space is needed attach a separate sheet. See instruction #1)* N/A	13. Sex [x] Male [ ] Female [ ] Non-Binary	14. Height 6 Feet 3 Inches	15. Weight 220 (lbs)	16. Eye Color [ ] Black [ ] Blue [ ] Brown [ ] Gray [x] Green [ ] Hazel [ ] Maroon [ ] Multiple [ ] Pink [ ] Other ______	17. Hair Color [ ] Bald [ ] Black [ ] Blond [ ] Brown [x] Gray [ ] Red [ ] Sandy [ ] White [ ] Other ______
	18. Ethnicity Hispanic or Latino [ ] Yes [x] No 19. Race *(Please check one or more boxes)* [ ] American Indian or Alaska Native [ ] Black or African American [ ] Native Hawaiian or Other Pacific Islander [ ] Asian [x] White				

For the following questions give full details on a separate sheet for all "Yes" answers *(see instruction #1)*	Yes	No
20. Have you ever held a Federal Firearms License? *(If so, please include FFL#)*		✔
21. Have you ever been a Responsible Person on a Federal Firearms License? *(If so, please include FFL#)* 1-22-333-22-22-55555	✔	
22. Have you ever been an officer in a corporation holding a Federal Firearms License? *(If so, please include FFL#)* 1-22-333-22-22-55555	✔	
23. Have you ever been an employee of a Federal Firearms Licensee?	✔	
24. Have you ever been denied a Federal Firearms License?		✔
25. Have you ever had a Federal Firearms License revoked?		✔
26. Are you under indictment or information in any court for a felony, or any other crime, for which the judge could imprison you for more than one year, or are you a current member of the military who has been charged with violation(s) of the Uniform Code of Military Justice and whose charge(s) have been referred to a general court-martial? *(See definition #10)*		✔
27. Have you ever been convicted in any court, including a military court, for a felony, or any other crime, for which the judge could have imprisoned you for more than one year, even if you received a shorter sentence including probation? *(See definition #10)*		✔
28. Are you a fugitive from justice? *(See definition #11)*		✔
29. Are you under 21 years of age?		✔
30. Are you an unlawful user of, or addicted to, marijuana or any depressant, stimulant, narcotic drug, or any other controlled substance? **Warning: The use or possession of marijuana remains unlawful under Federal law regardless of whether it has been legalized or decriminalized for medicinal or recreational purposes in the state where you reside.**		✔
31. Have you ever been adjudicated as a mental defective **OR** have you ever been committed to a mental institution? *(See definitions #12 and #13)*		✔
32. Have you been discharged from the Armed Forces under **dishonorable** conditions?		✔
33. Are you subject to a court order restraining you from harassing, stalking, or threatening your child or an intimate partner or child of such partner? *(See definition #5)*		✔
34. Have you ever been convicted in any court of a misdemeanor crime of domestic violence? *(See definition #7)*		✔

ATF Copy - Page 3

ATF Form 7(5310.12)/7CR(5310.16)
Revised October 2020

FFL Application Page 3

35. Country of Citizenship: *(Check/List more than one, if applicable. Nationals of the United States may check U.S.A.)*

☑ United States of America ☐ Other Country/Countries *(specify)*: ____________

	Yes	No
36. Have you ever renounced your United States citizenship?		✔
37. Are you an alien illegally or unlawfully in the United States?		✔
38. a. Are you an alien who has been admitted to the United States under a nonimmigrant visa? *(See definition #8)*		✔
b. If you are such an alien, do you fall within any of the exceptions stated in definition #9? Attach supporting documentation to the application. *(U.S. citizens/nationals leave 38b blank)*		

39. If you are an alien, record your U.S.-Issued Alien or Admission number *(AR#, USCIS#, or I94#)*: N/A

40. Under the penalties imposed by 18 U.S.C. § 924 and 1001, I declare that I have examined any related documents submitted in regard to this questionnaire/ATF Form 7/7CR Part B, and to the best of my knowledge and belief, they are true, correct and complete. This signature, when presented by a duly authorized representative of the U.S. Department of Justice, will constitute consent and authority for the appropriate U.S. Department of Justice representative to examine and obtain copies and abstracts of records and to receive statements and information regarding my background. Specifically, I hereby authorize the release of the following data or records to ATF: Military information/records, medical information/records, police and criminal records.

[signature]	Jim John Smith	11/01/2020
Signature	Printed Name	Date

EACH RESPONSIBLE PERSON MUST COMPLETE AND SIGN A SEPARATE QUESTIONNAIRE/ATF FORM 7/7CR PART B

Attach a 2" X 2" Photograph Here

If you are applying for a Type 03 ONLY a photograph is not required

1. Photo must have been taken within the last six months.
2. Photo must have been taken in full face view without a hat or head covering that obscures the hair or hairline.
3. On back of photograph print full name, last 4 of SSN, and business address.

Jim John Smith

Print Full Name

If applying for a NEW FFL:

Mail application, fingerprint cards, photographs, and application fees, including a separate questionnaire/Part B for EACH Responsible Person, to:

Federal Firearms Licensing Center
P.O. Box 6200-20
Portland, OR 97228-6200

If only adding a RP to an existing FFL:

Each Reponsible Person being added must complete a separate questionnaire/ATF Form 7/7CR Part B and mail it, along with their fingerprint card and photograph, to: ATF, Attn: FFLC, 244 Needy Rd, Martinsburg, WV 25405. Each questionnaire must be accompanied by a signed written request from a current/existing RP on the license, giving permission to add the Responsible Person.

Type 03 Applicants:

A photograph and fingerprint card are not required if you are applying for a Type 03 Collector of Curios and Relics license only.

Questions:

If you have any questions relating to this form, please contact the ATF Federal Firearms Licensing Center at 1-866-662-2750, or your local ATF Industry Operations Office.

Paperwork Reduction Act Notice

This request is in accordance with the Paperwork Reduction Act of 1995. The information collection is used to determine the eligibility of the applicant to engage in certain operations, to determine the location and extent of operations, and to determine whether the operations will be in conformity with Federal laws and regulations. The information requested is required in order to obtain or retain a benefit and is mandatory by statute *(18 U.S.C. § 923)*.

The estimated average burden associated with this collection of information is 60 minutes per respondent or recordkeeper, depending on individual circumstances. Comments concerning the accuracy of this burden estimate and suggestions for reducing this burden should be directed to Reports Management Officer, Resource Management Staff, Bureau of Alcohol, Tobacco, Firearms and Explosives, Washington, DC 20226.

An agency may not conduct or sponsor, and a person is not required to respond to, a collection of information unless it displays a currently valid OMB control number.

ATF Copy - Page 4

ATF Form 7(5310.12)/7CR(5310.16)
Revised October 2020

FFL Application Page 4

Chapter 13

Photographs

In this chapter, we're going to cover:

- **Responsible person photos**
- **Photo requirements**
- **Instructions for attaching to your application**

Responsible Person Photos

You will need to get a recent (last 6 months) 2×2″ photograph – this will go to the ATF along with Copy 1 of your FFL Application. Additionally, each Responsible Person listed on your application will also have to submit a photograph of theirselves to the ATF so make sure that they know they need to get one too!

Step 1. Get Your Photos

These photos are effectively passport photos. Yes, you are allowed to take and print your own photos at home, but unless you have the right equipment (good backdrop, photo quality printer, etc.) I encourage you to go get them taken at a local drugstore (Walgreen's, CVS, Rite Aid, etc.). They should cost you about $10 to have them professionally done. I understand that you may not want to spend the money on something that can be easily done at home but this is your first impression with the ATF – try to make it a good one!

Remember, you have no right to have an FFL. Right or wrong, you are working to convince the ATF that you are a responsible person who is worthy of the responsibility that comes with being an FFL. A quality photo goes a long way with making that impression.

If you want to take your own photos, or you want to ensure that the photos you purchased are sufficient, I suggest following the guidelines from the U.S. Department of State (below) for passport photos. As a note, even they recommend professional photos to prevent delays in passport applications.

NOTE: You and each Responsible Person on your application should each write your names on the back of your photos. This way, if they fall off or get mixed up, the ATF will know who is who.

Step 2. Attach Your Photos

Tape your photo in the appropriate spot on Copy 1 of your FFL Application. For your Responsible Persons, I suggest paper-clipping their photo to their fingerprint card.

U.S. Department of State Passport Photo Requirements

Your passport photo must be:

- In color
- Printed on matte or glossy photo quality paper
- 2 x 2 inches (51 x 51 mm) in size
- Sized such that the head is between 1 inch and 1 3/8 inches (between 25 and 35 mm) from the bottom of the chin to the top of the head. View the Photo Composition Template for more size requirement details.
- Taken within the last 6 months to reflect your current appearance
- Taken in front of a plain white or off-white background
- Taken in full-face view directly facing the camera
- Taken with a neutral facial expression (preferred) or a natural smile, and with both eyes open

- Taken in clothing that you normally wear on a daily basis:
    - Uniforms, clothing that looks like a uniform, and camouflage attire should not be worn in photos except in the case of religious attire that is worn daily.
    - You may only wear a hat or head covering if you wear it daily for religious purposes. Your full face must be visible and your head covering cannot obscure your hairline or cast shadows on your face.
    - Headphones, wireless hands-free devices or similar items are not acceptable in your photo.
    - If you normally wear prescription glasses, a hearing device or similar articles, they may be worn for your photo. Glare on glasses is not acceptable in your photo.
    - Dark glasses or non-prescription glasses with tinted lenses are not acceptable unless you need them for medical reasons (a medical certificate may be required).

Photo Composition Template:

Make sure the photo presents the full head from the top of the hair to the bottom of the chin

Center the head with the frame

The person in the photo should have a neutral expression and be facing the camera

Paper Photo Head Size Template:

Photo must be 2 inches by 2 inches

The height of the head (top of hair to bottom of chin) should measure 1 inch to 1 3/8 inches (25 mm – 35 mm)

Make sure the eye height is between 1 1/8 inches to 1 3/8 inches (28 mm – 35 mm) from the bottom of the photo

Photographer's Guide:

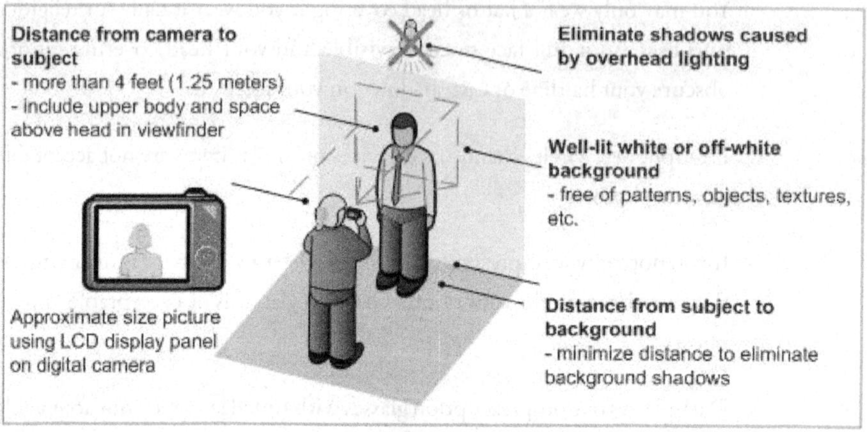

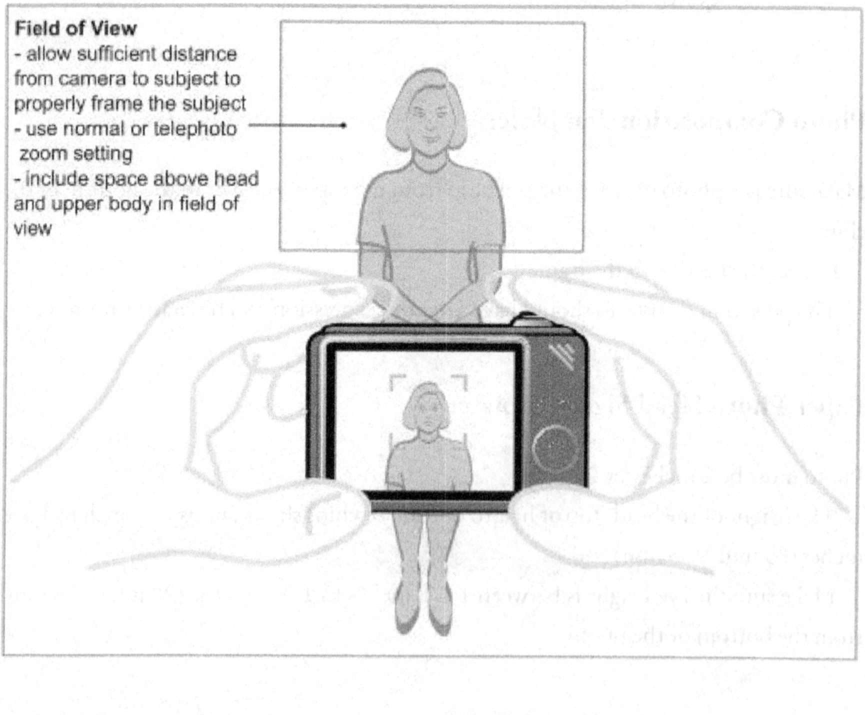

Acceptable Photo Examples:

Chapter 14

Fingerprint Cards

In this chapter, we're going to cover:

- **Fingerprint cards**
- **Instructions for completing fingerprint cards**

Fingerprint Cards

Each person on the FFL Application (you and each Responsible Person) will need to submit one completed fingerprint card. The fingerprint card must be the blue FD-258 card.

Previously, these fingerprint cards needed to be completed by a law enforcement agency, however, they have recently begun allowing fingerprints to be completed by anyone that is "capable" of doing so.

Of course, you can still use a law enforcement entity if you like – if so your local police station is your best spot to get these done. Call ahead to see what you'll need to bring with you (cash vs. check, forms of identification, etc.), what their hours are, and where to go once you're there. Most times you'll be going into a place where you are not permitted to carry weapons – plan ahead and leave your pocket knife and handgun in the car.

You can get your fingerprint cards from one of 3 sources:

1. Ordered directly from the ATF,
2. At whichever location you have your fingerprints done (they usually have plenty on-hand), or

3. Order from Amazon.com: FBI Fingerprint Cards, Form FD-258, 3 pack[1]

If you pick your fingerprint card up at the local police station, some of the information may not be correct. Don't worry, you can cross out the incorrect information with a BLACK pen and modify it so that it is correct.

Step 1. Have Fingerprints Taken

Please note that I don't have you start by filling out the information. This is for two reasons. First, many modern fingerprint systems use a scanner and printer instead of ink on your fingers. These printers often print the information on the card for you. Second, whoever is taking your fingerprints may want to see you fill out some or all of the information. This is not a requirement, but I've seen it happen. So, you should review the instructions below before you go so that you are prepared to fill out the information there.

Make sure that you have your fingerprint card(s) signed by the person who took your fingerprints before you leave!

Step 2. Fill Out Information Blocks on Fingerprint Cards

Fill out the following in BLACK ink ONLY!

Last Name, First Name, Middle Name. Include your full name. If you have no middle name, write "NMN"

Signature of person fingerprinted. Definitely wait to fill this out until you have your fingerprints taken. Often, the person taking the fingerprints wants to see you sign the card.

Aliases. If you have 'em, list 'em.

ORI. Add, or modify, this section to read "WVATF1100 ATF-FFLC Martinsburg, WV"

Date of Birth. MM/DD/YYY

Residence of Person Fingerprinted. This is your home address. Make sure your identification is up to date so that you don't have an issue with a mis-matched address.

Citizenship. Country of citizenship.

Sex. M/F

1. Available by following the URL/QR Code in the Introduction section.

Race. Use the letter code from the following chart. Each of these charts and codes are from the FBI's instructions for these cards.

Code	Race
A	Asian or Pacific Islander
B	Black
I	American Indian or Alaskan Native
U	Unknown
W	White or Hispanic

HGT. From the FBI, "Height must be expressed in feet and inches. Fractions of an inch should be rounded off to the nearest inch. Inches less than ten should be preceded by a zero. For example, five feet four inches should be submitted as "504" and six feet even should be submitted as "600"."

WGT. Enter your weight in pounds.

Eyes. Use the three letter code from the following chart.

Code	Color
BLK	Black
BLU	Blue
BRO	Brown
GRY	Grey
GRN	Green
HAZ	Hazel
MAR	Maroon

Hair. Use the three letter code from the following chart.

Code	Color
BLD	Bald
BLK	Black
BLN	Blonde
BLU	Blue
BRO	Brown
GRN	Green
GRY	Gray
ONG	Orange
PLE	Purple
PNK	Pink
RED	Red
SDY	Sandy
WHI	White
XXX	Unknown

Place of Birth. City and state of birth.

Date. Date of fingerprints.

Signature of Official Taking Fingerprints. Don't leave without making sure that they signed your card!

Your OCA. Leave Blank

Employer and Address. You can either leave this blank or put your company name and licensed premises address from your FFL application here. This block is meant for government hires and background checks – they want to know what agency or contractor the potential employee works for. In your case, they are not concerned with this information but you may choose to include it.

FBI No. Leave blank

Armed Forces No. Leave blank

Reason Fingerprinted. Write "FFL Application"

Social Security No. Include your social in the standard format: 123-45-6789

Miscellaneous No. Leave blank

Chapter 15

Application Checklist

The following is just your checklist to ensure that you have everything you need.

In the next chapter, I'll address where these go.

Please follow this checklist exactly as it appears – I can't count how many times I get questions like "Do I include fingerprint cards with the packet to the CLEO?" The answer to that questions, of course, is "No. Only the CLEO copy of the applicaiton goes to the CLEO."

1. Packet to ATF

INCLUDE:

- Application for FFL, Part A, ATF Copy (Form 7 / 5310.12)
- Completed Part B, ATF Copy (Form 7 / 5310.12) for each RP
- 2×2″ Photograph for each RP
- Fingerprint Card (FD-258) for each RP
- If you decided to pay by check: Check payable to "ATF" for amount selected in Question 10 of Application

2. Envelope to Chief Law Enforcement Officer (CLEO)

INCLUDE:

- Application for FFL, CLEO Copy (Form 7 / 5310.12)

Chapter 16

Application Submission

Now that your application materials are complete, it's time to put them in the mail.

Send your packet and your envelope to the following destinations.

1. Packet to ATF:

MAIL TO:

Federal Firearms Licensing Center
P.O. Box 6200-20
Portland, OR 97228-6200

2. Envelope to CLEO:

MAIL TO:

Your local Chief Law Enforcement Officer

This is either:

1. Your Chief of Police of your city/town,

2. Your Sheriff of your county, or

3. Your Chief of the state police.

You're Done!

Once your materials are in the mail, you have now officially completed your application for your FFL!

Congratulations!

After this step, you're done for a little while and you get to wait on the ATF to process your paperwork.

Take a break – you deserve it!

While you're waiting, it's a great time to start learning about all of the requirements you just signed up for. The next section introduces some of the firearms compliance areas that you need to be aware of. Be warned, it is only a basic review of the things you must know.

Chapter 17

Approval Process / Timeline

In this chapter, we're going to cover:

- **Application Approval Process**
- **Expected Approval Timeline**

Once your materials are in the mail, you have now officially completed your application for your FFL!

After this step, you're done for a little while, and you get to wait on the ATF to process your paperwork.

If you haven't sent your application in yet, stop reading and do so now. I appreciate you going ahead to learn more, but I don't want you to get this far and then delay submitting your application.

Application Process

Once the ATF receives your application, they'll process your payment and move it to the right area in the ATF for review.

Once it passes initial review, and they've confirmed that there are no errors on your application, they'll start the background check process (unless you're already cleared as an RP on another FFL).

After satisfying the background check requirements and having a properly completed application, ATF headquarters will reach out to your local field division to hand off your application.

A local investigator called an Industry Operations Investigator (IOI), will continue to review your application. This includes confirming anything with local law enforcement and looking at your intent and zoning issues.

The IOI will then contact you to schedule an initial inspection where the IOI will see your premises, discuss requirements with you, and clear up any issues with your application. You can prepare for this meeting with the information in Chapter 6 – Initial ATF Inspection

After a successful initial inspection, the IOI will then finish the process by giving their recommendation to ATF headquarters.

If approved, you should expect your FFL soon.

Application Timeline

On average, you can expect to have your FFL in your hands in 8 weeks.

Of course, sometimes the timeline can vary.

In about 6 weeks, you should expect to be contacted by an IOI.

If 8 weeks have passed without hearing anything after submission, you can call the licensing division (866-662-2750) to check on your application.

After your initial inspection, you should expect to have your FFL within another couple of weeks.

BASIC FIREARM COMPLIANCE

This section covers BASIC firearm compliance.

This book is focused on getting you your license – if you'd like more training in a specific area or you'd like to hire me as your firearms attorney, you can learn more by following the URL / QR Code in the Introduction Section (also included below):

https://rocketffl.com/book1

Chapter 18

Introduction

In this chapter, we're going to cover:

- **Introduction to firearm compliance**
- **Differences between laws, rules, and regulations**

Introduction to Basic Firearm Compliance

There are many laws, regulations, and rules you must follow as an FFL. If you're taking these chapters while you wait for the ATF to process your application - you are already on the right path! This means that you are aware that there's special requirements that you must follow and you're interested in learning about them before you get started as an FFL. "Compliance" is simply following the rules and you can't follow the rules if you don't know what they are. Good work on taking the first step to being compliant.... learning the rules.

Unfortunately, there is way more to cover than we can learn and master in just one section in a book on getting your FFL. As I'm going to keep mentioning, I offer much more training on these areas of compliance. The following info is just enough to get you started - you must learn more about each area. Please remember that the goal of this book is to help you get your FFL and get it set up the right way – for example, I think this is similar to getting education in "driver's ed" to get your driver's license, this is NOT an advanced course on how to drive a semi-truck or how to be a race-car driver. This is getting you your license – if you'd like more training in a specific area, it's available.

If you choose to learn more with me, or perhaps want legal support before or during ATF issues, you can learn more about the additional training I offer and you can explore hiring me as your attorney by following the URL / QR Code in the Introduction Section.

Firearm compliance is more than just "ATF Compliance." For example, there are also unique import/export rules and local (State/County/City) laws that FFLs must follow.

Laws, Regulations, and Rules

Each of these things relies on the others and all must be followed. The law set out the main requirement, the regulation allows the federal agency to ensure that the law is being followed, and the rule helps guide how the regulation may be followed.

Laws

Simply, laws are things that have been created and passed by a legislative body and then signed into law by an executive. For example, Congress creates and passes a bill and then the President signs it into law. Laws are the foundation of the rules we must follow. The 3 most prominent areas of law that are going to affect your life as an FFL are the National Firearms Act of 1934 (NFA), the Gun Control Act of 1968 (GCA), and the Arms Export Control Act (AECA).

Even though the GCA was created later than the NFA, the GCA is referred to as "Title I" of federal firearms law and the NFA is referred to as "Title II." This is why you'll hear NFA firearms, such as silencers or full-auto machine-guns, also referred to as "Title II" firearms.

Regulations

Agencies are parts of government created to help enforce the laws. On a federal level, the Bureau of Alcohol, Tobacco, Firearms, and Explosives (ATF) is an agency created to enforce federal firearms laws. Agencies are authorized to create their own regulations to help them enforce the laws. Although they aren't technically "laws," regulations must still be followed because they are created by the government to help carry-out the laws.

Rules

Rules are also something an agency creates. Rules help you to understand how the regulations may be followed. Although they are not laws nor regulations, they too must still be followed. They are simply guidance from the agency which helps regulations apply to certain situations. They are easier to change/update with changing technology or circumstances.

Example

As an example of how each of these works, the law makes it illegal for "prohibited persons" to possess firearms in 18 U.S.C. § 922(g). The "U.S.C" stands for "United States Code." Whenever you see "code," you know it's a law. The "§" symbol means "section."

ATF has enacted regulations that require a purchaser of a firearm from an FFL to fill out a specific form (the Form 4473) that has questions on it to determine whether someone is a "prohibited person" in 27 C.F.R. § 478.124. "C.F.R." stands for "Code of Federal Regulations."

The ATF has further made a rule that allows FFLs to use an electronic, instead of handwritten on paper, version of a Form 447 in ATF Ruling 2016-2.

Chapter 19

ATF Compliance

In this chapter, we're going to cover:

- **ATF firearm compliance**
- **Firearm traces and records**
- **Violations**
- **GCA vs. NFA**
- **Facility requirements**
- **Employees and training**
- **Firearm and parts imports**

Again, this is merely a basic overview of ATF compliance. As I'll continue to remind you, you should get specific training in ATF Compliance by following the URL / QR code in the introduction section.

Traceability

If I could summarize ATF compliance into one word, it would be this: Traceability.

The motivation behind almost every ATF regulation and rule is the ability to trace a firearm if it is ever used in a crime. This means that, as an FFL, you are an important step in the ATF's ability to prevent and solve crimes with firearms - you must take your job seriously!

If a gun is recovered from a crime, the ATF will "trace" the firearm. Contrary to popular belief, there is no firearm-owner database (this is a good thing!).

First, the ATF will contact the manufacturer to see when and where the firearm was made and then where it was sent. This requires that there are proper markings on the firearm so that it can be identified and that the manufacturer keeps proper records. The ATF will then go down the line from FFL to FFL and track where the firearm was received and sent until it was sold to a customer (non-FFL). This requires that each distributor and dealer have accurate records. Then, the ATF will get the information from the Form 4473 filled out by the FFL and customer to find where the gun left the FFL-system and then contact that person. This too requires accurate records.

If any one of the steps is broken because of inaccurate markings or records, then the ATF won't be able to trace the firearm. This means that if you aren't compliant, you may prevent the ATF from helping to solve a crime. Or worse, if you sell a firearm to someone who shouldn't have had one in the first place, you may have helped contribute to the crime taking place.

Traceability is an important concept to remember. Even without knowing every law, rule, or regulations (you should), you can ask yourself whether what you're about to do will hinder ATF's ability to trace a firearm. If it will, then you probably shouldn't do it.

Records

Most of your work involving ATF compliance is record-keeping. You need to keep track of the firearms you make/receive and the firearms you sell/ship/destroy in your Acquisition and Disposition (A&D) log. You must track information about each customer, the results of a background check (if needed), and firearm details on your Form 4473s. You must report multiple purchases of handguns and, in some states, certain rifles on Multiple Sales Forms. You must file special paperwork upon the theft/loss of a firearm within 48 hours of knowing it was loft/stolen and manufacturers must submit an annual manufacturing report. Each of these types of records is discussed later.

If you're not good at keeping records, either get good or get someone to help you! Your operation as an FFL and your obligation to help ATF prevent and solve crimes depends on it!

Violations

If the ATF learns of your non-compliance, either through an inspection or in connection with an investigation, you will be cited for violating the relevant law or regulation. I often hear clients of mine say things like, "I just transferred a firearm without conducting a background check, I'm not a criminal!" Well, technically they are - failing to follow the laws or regulations is a crime!

So, what happens when you receive a citation? It depends. If it is your first inspection and the violations are fairly minor and the ATF believes that they were honest mistakes and that you can fix them, then you'll likely receive the citations with only a warning to improve. If the problems continue, or if they are serious enough, the ATF can revoke your license or even prosecute you.

Note that even relatively minor violations, if continued, can be treated as severely as a relatively major violation. You're most likely to get into trouble for "willful violations" of the law. If you knew better and have already been warned about something and you kept doing it, then it is no longer a mistake, it is a "willful violation" and you can get into serious trouble. This doesn't mean that you are always going to get a warning before it becomes a repeat violation. You have an obligation as an FFL to know and comply with all the laws, rules, and regulations. Also, during your initial inspection to get your FFL (covered in the next section) you're going to initial and sign a form which says you've been told about all of your requirements and that you agree to abide by them.

Don't mistake my reference to "minor violations" above to think that small problems are ok. They are not! In fact, even a typo on one of your records can be seen as a "willful violation" and could lead to you losing your license, or worse, your freedom. I wrote an article for the National Shooting Sports Foundation (NSSF) titled "Sweat the Details"[1] which helps to explain why strict compliance is important and how even typos can get you into trouble.

GCA vs NFA

The ATF enforces both the Gun Control Act (GCA) and the National Firearms Act (NFA). These two sets of laws cover different types of firearms. The GCA covers "standard" firearms such as rifle, shotguns, and handguns. The NFA covers "special" firearms like silencers, machine guns, and short-barreled-rifles. There is some overlap, however. For

1. Available at the URL / QR Code in the Introduction Section.

example, NFA firearms (including silencers) are still firearms which are covered by both sets of laws.

Having your FFL allows you to operate with GCA/Title I firearms. You may still possess NFA/Title II firearms in certain situations but you'll need to Become a Special Occupational Taxpayer (SOT) in order to engage in business (selling/making) with NFA/Title II firearms.

These two sections of the law have their own very unique requirements. For example, a GCA firearm may simply be transferred to another FFL by logging the transfer into your A&D record whereas special permission is required from the ATF before you may transfer an NFA firearm.

For more info on the firearms covered by these laws, what these laws require, and how to comply with them, see the extra resources I've linke in the URL / QR Code in the Introduction Section on ATF Compliance.

Licensed Premises

You may only conduct business at your licensed location. Your FFL must be displayed on the wall along with the Youth Handgun safety notice that the ATF will give you during your initial inspection. The exceptions to this are certain events allowed by law (most gun shows) and employees who have a firearm off-site for a bona-fide business purpose (discussed below). There are other requirements as well, such as having firearm locks available for purchase at your premises.

Security

You must maintain reasonable security. There is no specific requirement for precise security measures. For example, there's no requirement that you keep your guns locked up in a safe. However, and especially if you don't lock your firearms in a safe, you need to have a good alarm system and you should have good reinforcements on windows and doors. You have a responsibility to keep your firearms out of the hands of criminals. The ATF is going to determine whether your security is reasonable by taking a look around during your initial inspection.

If you get broken into and robbed, it isn't your fault. However, if the ATF determines that you didn't do anything to help prevent a robbery, your license can be in jeopardy.

Manufacturers

If you make 50 firearms or more in a year, then you also must pay a special excise tax to the Tax and Trade Bureau (TTB). The tax is calculated only on certain parts of the firearm. For more information on this, see our book on ATF Compliance.

This isn't really "ATF" compliance but this was the best place I could find for this information.

Employees

Employees of your FFL are allowed to, in some ways, act as the FFL. For example, when a salesperson takes a firearm off the wall to show to a customer, the FFL is still in possession of the firearm. Also, when the employee is selling the firearm and completing the Form 4473 with the customer and conducting a background check (if needed), they are acting as the FFL and must follow all the same requirements.

It is important to note that an employee must be an actual bona-fide employee. Sub-contractors or friends/family helping you out are not necessarily bona-fide employees and are therefore not permitted to act as the FFL. If you're paying the employee via a W-2, then they're an actual employee.

A bona-fide employee may actually leave your licensed premises with a firearm on your A&D record for a legitimate business purpose without it being counted as a transfer to an individual. This type of off-site possession is called a "temporary assignment" and the firearm is considered to still be in your inventory even though it is not present at your location. An example of this would be a salesperson who takes a firearm to an event to demonstrate the firearm for sale. This does not include an employee taking the firearm home because they like it.

A mentioned above, you may not employ Prohibited Persons. Also, if your employee is able to manage your facility and make compliance-related decisions, there's a good chance that they are a Responsible Person (RP) and should be listed as such on your FFL. The ATF looks at it like this: an employee doesn't need to be/isn't an RP if they are supervised by an RP. If however, they are able to make the decision whether to continue with a certain transaction then they might be an RP. The ATF trusts RPs to supervise employees. If the employee can do something to interfere with compliance without supervision (i.e. they are probably an RP) and you don't have them listed as an RP, then the ATF will view this as you preventing them from vetting a potential bad person who has the capability to do bad things (e.g. sell guns out the back door without paperwork).

Training

The ATF requires that everyone acting on behalf of your FFL is knowledgeable about the requirements. It doesn't help if you know whats right and wrong if your employee makes a mistake. You will still receive a violation for everything your employees do or fail to do.

Your employees should be trained on their first day on the job and you should continue to train them. Of course, you are welcome to have your employees take all of my training on ATF Compliance, however, that generally isn't necessary. Instead, I have much simpler and shorter training for employees of retailers and manufacturers that you can find at the URL / QR Code in the Introduction Section. The retailer version focuses on retail-specific issues like Form 4473s while the manufacturer version focuses on manufacturer-specific issues like firearm determinations (when a piece of material becomes a firearm) and firearm markings.

I strongly encourage you to sit each new employee (and your current employees, if any) down and make them take their respective training. Also, the training has a quiz at the end to measure the employee's understanding of ATF compliance. Upon successful completion of the training, each employee will receive an official certificate of completion that can be placed in their file to show that they've been trained. This will help you to hold them accountable and it will go a long way to show the ATF that you take compliance seriously should a mistake ever happen.

Imports

The ATF regulates all imports of firearms and ammunition. Exports are covered under U.S. State Department/Dept. of Commerce Compliance.

In addition to firearms and ammunition, the ATF also regulates the import of "defense articles." Defense articles are also discussed along with exports in U.S. State Department/Dept. of Commerce Compliance. For now, just know that this means that the ATF regulates the imports of firearm parts as well as complete firearms.

Prior to the import of firearms, firearm parts, or ammunition, an ATF Form 6 must be submitted for approval to the ATF. Upon approval, the ATF will return an ATF Form 6A. This approved form will allow for the import of the requested items. The exception to this is any firearm parts under $100 in value. Note: you may not break up larger shipments into smaller shipments under $100 to avoid the approval process through the ATF. Be extremely careful here - it is easy to mistakenly violate this requirement.

For example, if you order a rifle stock off of a website and don't pay attention to the fact that the company is located in Canada and the rifle stock is shipping from Canada, then you might violate some serious firearm import laws without meaning to. This is because a rifle stock counts as a "defense article" and if it is over $100 in value, then you must submit an ATF Form 6 and receive an approved ATF Form 6A prior to importing the stock into the United States. Also, you must ensure that the export laws of Canada are being followed. While their laws don't govern you, your stock might get held up in transit if it is seized by the Canadian government.

Let this be a lesson: compliance doesn't just keep you out of trouble with the law, it also allows you to run a business!

If you can't get your firearms or parts, you can't run your business. I've heard the following from clients before, "I don't care if my vendor doesn't follow the rules, that's their problem." Wrong! If your vendor gets shut down, you've just lost your supply of parts and you may have contraband that you'll need to surrender, or worse, recall items from your customers.

You may order firearms or parts from a foreign company as long as they import the goods into the United States properly and ship you only the goods that they already imported through someone else.

Also, there are other considerations (e.g. Customs, labeling the foreign source) that you'll need to look out for when importing products to this country.

Chapter 20

US Dept of State / Dept Commerce Compliance

In this chapter, we're going to cover:

- **Export compliance**
- **Dept. of State vs. Dept. of Commerce**
- **What is an export?**
- **ITAR manufacturing**
- **Employees and training**

Export Compliance

Even if you don't plan on exporting firearms, you should pay attention to this chapter. As you'll find out, you might have an export in your gun shop without even realizing it.

Also, export controls, especially topics concerning "ITAR," are greatly misunderstood in our community and rule changes in 2020 have significantly changed things.

You might need to register as a "manufacturer" with the U.S. Department of State under ITAR even if you don't need a Manufacturer's FFL. However, the likelihood of this is MUCH slimmer after the 2020 changes. Previously, failing to register under ITAR was one thing I could predict would be an issue when I worked with a smaller manufacturer. Now, ITAR registration won't be an issue for the vast majority of firearms businesses.

The Arms Export Control Act (AECA) governs the export of firearms, ammunition, and other defense articles. There are two federal agencies that regulate the AECA - the U.S. Department of State (State) and the U.S. Department of Commerce (Commerce). As mentioned in the previous chapter, a third agency regulates AECA but mainly only regarding imports.

This is an extremely basic overview of export compliance - if you're looking for more information, please consider looking into training on Export Compliance.

Export Control Reform

Prior to the big changes for the export control of firearms and ammunition in 2020, the firearms industry was significantly burdened by export controls - even in situations where an export might never occur.

For example, the following scenarios used to apply (they are no longer valid):

If you were a non-FFL machine shop that made handgun or rifle parts (not receivers), you'd have to register under ITAR and pay an annual fee.

If you had a Type 07 manufacturers FFL that only "occasionally" assembled, AR-15s, although you were a manufacturer for ATF purposes, you weren't for State purposes and therefore didn't need to register as a manufacturer under ITAR.

If you were a Type 01 FFL gunsmith, and you wanted to re-barrel a customer's rifle or tap and thread a receiver for a scope, then you'd have to register as a manufacturer under ITAR, but you didn't need a manufacturer's FFL under ATF rules.

As you can imagine, there was a lot of confusion about ITAR registration and surprise when people who never intended to export, nor realized they needed to register because they didn't consider themselves a "manufacturer", got into trouble with State over ITAR issues.

The changes in our export control reform did not change the rules for each agency. Instead, the changes moved certain firearms, parts, and ammunition out from under U.S. Dept. of State control (ITAR) and moved them over to the jurisdiction of the U.S. Department of Commerce. Therefore, ITAR rules still apply - they just apply to fewer products.

Yes, it may have been clearer to only include here what the rules are instead of what they used to be, however, there is so much confusion here, I think that it is important to explain what happened.

State vs. Commerce

The US Dept of State used to regulate the export of handguns, rifles, and shotguns with barrels under 18 inches in length (Short Barreled Shotguns) and Commerce only regulated shotguns with barrels equal to or greater than 18 inches.

Now, however, most all firearms, parts, and ammunition have been moved from State to Commerce. In addition to these firearms, each agency also regulates the parts, ammunition, and some information concerning these items (covered below) for the firearms under their jurisdiction.

U.S. Department of State (State)

Within State, there's a division which oversees the regulations created by State regarding exports of arms - this division is called the Directorate of Defense Trade Controls (DDTC). The regulations that State created and which are overseen by DDTC are called the International Traffic in Arms Regulations (ITAR). The ITAR sets forth rules for registration, licensing of exports, and foreign agreements of certain items and certain information concerning the items.

These items are on a list in the ITAR called the United States Munitions List (USML). Items on this list include various arms and military-grade equipment.

Previously rifles, handguns, silencers, and short barreled shotguns (and, of book, their parts and ammo) were all on the USML and therefore fell under ITAR.

After the export control reform change in 2020, however, only a few items in the firearms industry remain on the USML:

- Full-auto machineguns,
- Caseless ammunition,
- Tracer ammunition,
- Silencers / Suppressors,
- Drum magazines with over 50 round capacity,
- Linked/belted ammunition,
- Parts specific to such items, and

- some more nuanced/rarer items

U.S. Department of Commerce (Commerce)

Within Commerce, there's a division that oversees the regulations by Commerce regarding exports - this division is called the Bureau of Industry and Security (BIS). The regulations that Commerce created and are overseen and enforced by BIS are called the Export Administration Regulations (EAR). The EAR sets forth rules for licensing of exports of certain items and certain information concerning the items.

These items are on a list in the EAR called the Commerce Control List (CCL). Items on this list used to only include:

Shotguns with barrels 18 inches or longer in length and their parts/components.

However, with the items moved over from State under the export control reform initiative, the CCL now contains:

- All non-full-auto rifles,
- All non-full-auto shotguns,
- All non-full-auto handguns,
- All parts and ammunition for those firearms, and
- Everything else (e.g. pencils and toilet paper).

As you can imagine, it might be difficult to determine whether a shotgun part belongs to a shotgun regulated under State or Commerce. Or, whether a screw is regulated as a part of a rifle under State or as part of a microwave under Commerce. Determinations over who has jurisdiction can be requested through a special process called a Commodity Jurisdiction (CJ) request. Some items are considered "Dual-Use" and are covered under Commerce if they have a commercial use and military use.

If you're interested in how to determine how certain items are controlled, which items are under which jurisdiction (for example, which scopes are "military-grade"), and how to get proper licensing or permits for these items or information, you should take our book on Export Compliance (coming soon.)

What is an Export?

First, we need to cover what an export is. Here's a hint: it's probably not what you think. As you'll find out, an export isn't necessarily something leaving the country. Instead, it is the receipt of items or information by a foreign person - even while they are in the United States.

Under federal law, an export is:

Sending or taking something ("Defense Articles" under ITAR and firearms, dual-use items, and certain information under EAR are what we're concerned with for firearm export law) out of the United States

Disclosing (including oral or visual disclosure) or transferring technical data to a foreign person, **whether in the United States or abroad**.

Performing a defense service on behalf of, or for the benefit of, a foreign person, **whether in the United States or abroad**.

From those three definitions, we know a couple of things. First, in addition to "Defense Articles," things called "Technical Data" and "Defense Services" can also be exported. Second, "Technical Data" and "Defense Services" can be exported WITHOUT LEAVING THE UNITED STATES!

Clearly, it's important to know what these things are.

Defense Articles

A "Defense Article" is any item on the USML and the "Technical Data" for those items. This includes the firearms listed on the USML and also their parts and components. Some parts and components have stronger restrictions, such as barrels and receivers, and are referred to as Significant Military Equipment (SME).

Technical Data

"Technical Data" is information that is required for the design, development, production, manufacture, assembly, operation, repair, testing, maintenance, or modification of defense articles. There is an exemption for any information that is already available to the public. Therefore, if the information can already be found elsewhere, it likely isn't "Technical Data." You can not, however, put the information up on your website and then say that it is now publicly available.

This can be tricky. If you're a manufacturer, then your parts drawings, specifications, and even some unique machinery/processes are likely "Technical Data." If you allow a foreign person to see "Technical Data" then you have just made an export. If you did so without an export license, then you just broke the law. This is why you can't just publish "Technical Data" on your website in an attempt to make it publicly available. By putting it on your website, you've just allowed foreign persons to see it.

Defense Services

Providing a "Defense Service" is the furnishing of assistance (including training)... in the design, development, engineering, manufacture, production, assembly, testing, repair, maintenance, modification, operation, demilitarization, destruction, processing or use of defense articles.

This can also be tricky. Certain training on how to make, repair, or use firearms can be a "Defense Service." The same exemption for public information from "Technical Data" applies to "Defense Services." If you train a foreign person on something related to firearms that isn't publicly available without an export license, then you may have just broken the law.

Summary: Certain information relating to firearms can be exported when shared/shown/given to a foreign person - no matter where that person is located. If you want to learn more, look into our Export Compliance book.

Commerce does not have similar definitions. This is an important distinction and one of the great reasons for the export control reform initiative.

There is no "defense service" definition under Commerce, which effectively lifts much of the restrictions on training foreigners on how to use firearms. And, although there is also no "technical data" definition under Commerce, information and technology are still controlled and may not be exported without a permit. Therefore, training is only ok as long as no technical information is transferred (information about how to particularly make or develop the item).

Manufacturing

Even if you aren't a manufacturer for ATF purposes you might be one for State/ITAR purposes. This is because each agency is allowed to make its own regulations. As far as the ATF is concerned, you are only a manufacturer if you are actually making firearms. However, if you are making parts for firearms (Defense Articles) or if you are making certain modifications to firearms (which might only be considered gunsmithing by the ATF and only require a Type 1 FFL), then State considers you a manufacturer for ITAR purposes. ITAR-manufacturers must register with the DDTC.

The yearly fee for registration is **$3,000**. This fee increases if you've had any trouble or reviews with State. This fee also applies if you are a "broker" of an export.

Due to the confusion about what types of activities constituted "manufacturing" under ITAR, DDTC released some guidance in July of 2016. Although this guidance surely cleared up what the DDTC thought, it created a lot of confusion in the firearms industry. As you can see from the below list of activities that constitute manufacturing under ITAR, some of these activities are things that most people thought were only gunsmithing.

This is not much of an issue anymore after export control reform because most firearms and activities at issue have been moved over to commerce, however, the definitions still apply to any firearm or item left under ITAR control.

Again, the guidance below still applies to firearms under ITAR, which is NOT most firearms.

According to the July 2016 guidance from DDTC, the following activities require registration with State under ITAR:

Use of any special tooling or equipment upgrading in order to improve the capability of assembled or repaired firearms

Modifications to a firearm that change round capacity

The production of firearm parts (including, but not limited to, barrels, stocks, cylinders, breech mechanisms, triggers, silencers, or suppressors)

The systemized production of ammunition, including the automated loading or reloading of ammunition

The machining or cutting of firearms (e.g. threading of muzzles or muzzle brake installation requiring machining, that results in an enhanced capability)

Re-chambering firearms through machining, cutting, or drilling

Chambering, cutting, or threading barrel blanks

Blueprinting firearms by machining the barrel

The following activities do NOT require registration under ITAR:

Occasional assembly of firearm parts and kits that do not require cutting, drilling, or machining

Firearm repairs involving one-for-one drop-in replacement parts that do not require any cutting, drilling, or machining for installation

Repairs involving replacement parts that do not improve the accuracy, caliber, or other aspects of firearm operation

Hydrographic paint or Cerakote application or bluing treatments for a firearm

Attachment of accessories to a completed firearm without drilling, cutting, or machinings—such as attaching a scope, sling, or light to existing mounts or hooks, or attaching a flash suppressor, sound suppressor, muzzle brake, or similar item to a pre-threaded muzzle

Cosmetic additions and alterations (including engraving) that do not improve the accuracy, caliber, or other aspects of firearm operation beyond its original capabilities

Machining new dovetails or drilling and tapping new holes for the installation of sights, do not improve the accuracy or operation of the firearm beyond its original capabilities

Manual loading or reloading of ammunition of .50 caliber or smaller

How to Export

Exporting is a complicated process. If you are planning to export (including having a foreign person tour your facility), you should get professional assistance.

Visitors

You should be screening visitors if they are going to be likely to see Technical Data or receive a Defense Service. Checking identification and keeping a visitor's log that asks whether the visitor is a U.S. Person is a must for manufacturing facilities.

Employees

Just as with other areas of compliance, your employees must be trained. An employee on the range, at a gun show or trade show, or dealing with foreign customers might make an unlawful export without even knowing it. This affects both them and you and your business. Surely, they don't need to know as much about Export Compliance as you or your head of compliance do, but they should have an introductory book on what to watch out for. Therefore, we've made a condensed/introductory book just for employees, the Employee-level Export Compliance book.

Just like with ATF compliance training, I strongly encourage you to sit each new employee (and your current employees, if any) down and make them take their respective books. The books are inexpensive to encourage you to do this. Also, each book has a quiz at the end to measure the employee's understanding of export compliance. Upon successful completion of the book, each employee will receive an official certificate of completion that can be placed in their file to show that they've been trained. This will help you to hold them accountable, and it will go a long way to show State or Commerce that you take compliance seriously should a mistake ever happen.

Depending on your level of involvement, this area of compliance requires an actual export compliance plan, policies, and training.

Export Control Summary

Ok, we've got a lot to summarize for a review of what we've covered:

There are two federal agencies that regulate exports: State and Commerce.

The division of state that oversees its regulations and our industry is the DDTC or Directorate of Defense Trade Controls and for Commerce, it is the BIS or Bureau of Industry and Security.

Each of these regulations has a specific list of items that helps to determine how they are controlled. For State, the list is the USML or United Stated Munitions List and for Commerce, it is the CCL or Commerce Control List.

An export is:

Sending or taking something out of the country,

disclosing "technical data" to a foreign person, OR

performing a "defense service" for a foreign person

Technical data is any information that is NOT publicly available which can help someone make or operate a firearm. This includes drawings, specs, and special processes.

A "defense service" is providing non-publicly available training to a foreign person.

It is important to remember that exports can occur with technical data or a defense service even if it happens within our country!

Here's the best advice I can give you in this area - be extremely careful with foreign persons. Except for a few exceptions, they can not possess firearms in this country, and you can't let them see or hear technical data!

The last note here is that your employees MUST be trained - this protects you and them.

Chapter 21

Record Keeping

In this chapter, we're going to cover:

- **Record keeping**
- **Acquisition and disposition records**
- **Firearm transfer record (4473)**
- **Multiple sales forms**
- **FFLs, AFMER reports, Theft/Loss reports, and more**
- **Import/Export records**
- **Training**

Running a successful FFL requires great record keeping. Invest the time now to get yourself set up right. When an ATF inspection ultimately comes, you won't be stressed or panicked if your records are complete and in order.

Acquisition and Disposition (A&D) Records

Your Acquisition and Disposition (A&D) records are the most important record for all FFLs. These records sometimes called the "bound book" or simply the "book(s)," keep track of every gun you've received, currently have, and/or transferred to customers or other FFLs.

The easiest way to picture how these records work is to imagine an actual bound book laid out flat. The left page is the guns you've received (the acquisitions) and the right page is the guns you've sent out/let go (dispositions). When you've acquired a gun, you took possession of it and brought it onto your records. A line on the left page would then be completed showing the required details of the firearm. When you "disposed of" it, you didn't throw it away, rather you transferred it off of your records. The corresponding line on the right page for that firearm would then be completed with the necessary information about where the firearm went and how.

Once the disposition information is filled-in, the gun is out of your inventory. As long as the disposition information is blank, then the gun should still be in your inventory. These are sometimes referred to as "open dispositions." They're the records that ATF is going to use to confirm your inventory accuracy during an inspection.

There are many requirements for which information is required, and when it must be entered. Please keep in mind that this guide is a tool to walk you through the FFL application process only. For in-depth operational guidance, you'll need to sign up for the ATF Compliance program.

You can keep your bound book by hand on paper or electronically. Although I love computerized records, there is a simplicity in keeping your bound book as a handwritten physical book. If you are going to have low inventory numbers, don't expect to be completing many transactions, and/or don't want to hassle with computers/software/backups of files for your FFL, then I encourage you to purchase a physical bound book and keep your records by hand.

If you'd rather keep your A&D record electronically, you have two options:

1. Use an excel spreadsheet, or

2. Use specialized Bound Book software.

I used to recommend using a spreadsheet as a simple solution that was low cost (free). It was a risk, however, because it was on you to learn the right way to use it (and to actually keep up with the records properly).

The other alternative was to use paid FFL software but the downsides to that option are cost and even the best options out there seem clunky and require a lot of clicking around and menu navigation just to get them to work.

However, now, there's ZERO reason to use a spreadsheet or pay for clunky and outdated FFL Software - I made FFLSafe.com to be the best, cleanest, and simplest FFL Software to use for your A&D Book and it is 100% free.

If you choose to keep your bound book electronically, the ATF requires that semi-annually you download and store a copy at your licensed business premises. This can be done using a physical storage device, such as a USB flash drive, or a printout. If you're using a spreadsheet you'll have to remember to do this on your own and if you're using paid FFL software you'll probably have to go through a set-up process to get it syncing and working properly.

Or, if you chose FFLSafe.com, it is all done automatically for you.

Regardless of which option you choose, you must maintain your records correctly! There are many specific requirements for what information is entered, how the information must be entered when it must be entered, and how it must be corrected (if needed). Please consider taking a follow-on training on ATF compliance.

4473

7 out of the top 10 violations for FFLs during inspections are from the ATF Form 4473 ("4473"). This form is the record used to transfer a firearm to a non-FFL (customers). When completing a transaction with a non-FFL, a background check is generally required. There are some exemptions in certain states for concealed firearm license holders (CCWs). Also, depending on your state, you either call the FBI for the background check through the National Instant Criminal System (NICS) or you call an agency in your state for the background check. Learn more about this distinction in the chapter on State-Level Compliance.

There is way too much on this form to cover in an introductory chapter on basic compliance. For in-depth guidance, please refer to the extra compliance training.

I recommend using an electronic 4473. You'll be able to better catch common errors, and you won't have poor handwriting problems. If you're trying to get these records right by yourself, then you can fill out the forms by hand – the ATF will give you a small stack during your initial inspection, and you can order more as needed.

Of all the FFLSafe.com can do, I'm most proud of its electronic 4473 – I think it is hte simplest and easiest 4473 out there.

Multiple Sales Forms

For sales of multiple handguns within a 5 business-day period and certain rifles along with the Mexican-bordered states, a special multiple sales form must be submitted to the ATF and local law enforcement. This is a big one because it is often overlooked. This form must be sent to the ATF and local law enforcement. In addition to keeping a copy attached to the relevant 4473, you should always retain proof that you sent the form. Often, the ATF fails to keep track of these and if they lost their copy, they will accuse you of never sending it.

FFLs, AFMER Reports, Theft/Loss Reports, and others

There are many other forms and records utilized by FFLs, which are not covered in this book on getting your FFL.

FFLs

You must keep an unsigned copy of your FFL in your records and a signed copy on your wall in a conspicuous (easy to see/find) location.

AFMER Reports

Manufacturers and Exporters must keep records of each type of firearm manufactured so that they may submit their required Annual Firearm Manufacture and Export Report (AFMER).

Theft/Loss Reports

Theft/Loss reports to the ATF must be maintained ALONG with proof that you actually submitted the record.

Business records

You must have your business records on file for the ATF. These include your business registration, W-2 employee information, and more.

ATF Correspondence

All correspondence with the ATF must be retained. Your first correspondence for your FFL will be the actual application packet. Therefore....keep a copy of the application and attachment pages for your records!

Import/Export Records

There are very specific records for importers and exporters to keep. If you're looking on guidance how to do this, you need to take our book on Export Compliance and ATF Compliance (for imports). This is a HIGHLY specialized area - tread lightly.

Training Records

You should keep records of your and your employee's training. Not only will this help to show federal regulators (ATF, State, and Commerce) that you are making efforts to be compliant so that any slip-up must have been a mistake and not a conscious choice, it will also help if you ever need to separate one employee's bad actions from your company and FFL. If an employee does the wrong thing, and they knew better, then you did your part and the ATF will only be mad at them. However, if you didn't train them, or you were indifferent to their bad actions, then it will reflect poorly on the entire FFL.

Chapter 22

Record Keeping Quiz

Given the following information, how many errors can you find in the following A&D / Bound Book entry?

Scenario: You received 3 firearms on January 1st, 2016 – a Glock 19, a Remington 870, and a Springfield XD. The first two came from a distributor and the third came from a customer.

RocketFFL.com A&D Bound Book	Firearm Info				Acquisition	
Manufacturer and Importer (if any)	Model	Serial No.	Type	Caliber or Gauge	Receipt Date	Receipt Name and address
Glock	G19	12345678	Semi-auto	9mm	2/1/16	Lipseys 572033017A09424
Remington Arms Co.	870	23456789	Shotgun	12 Ga.	2/2/16	Lipseys 572033017A09424
Springfield	XD - .40 S&W	34567890	Pistol	.40 S&W	2/3/16	Joe Bob P.O. Box 123, Phoenix, AZ 85029

QUESTION: How many errors are in the above entries?

Answer on next page.

ANSWER: There were 10 errors in that sample record!

To be fair, I am assuming that you know some pretty specific details about these firearms. However, even if you don't know some of these off the top of your head, hopefully the answer below helps illuminate how much there is to learn and know.

[Glock] The Manufacturer name is wrong. It can only be either "Glock/Glock, Inc." or "Glock, Inc."

[Glock] The model is wrong. It must be "19" only

[Glock] The type is wrong. It must be "Pistol"

[Glock] The caliber is wrong. It should be 9x19

[Glock] The receipt date is wrong. It should be 1/1/16

[Remington] The receipt date is wrong. It should be 1/1/16

[Springfield] The manufacturer name is wrong. It should be "HS Product/Springfield Armory U.S.A."

[Springfield] The model is wrong. It should just be "XD"

[Springfield] The receipt date is wrong. It should be 1/1/16

[Springfield] The Receipt name and address is wrong. A P.O. Box is not a residence.

How did you do? Perhaps it's time to look into some ATF Firearms Compliance training?

Chapter 23

State-Level Compliance

In this chapter, we're going to cover:

- **Background Checks (NICS vs. POC)**
- **State-Specific Rules**

Background Checks (NICS vs. POC)

Depending on your state, you either use the federal NICS system for background checks, a state-level agency for background checks, or a combination of the two.

When a state conducts its own background checks, it is referred to as a "Point of Contact" ("POC") state. If all transactions go through the state, it is called a full-POC state. If only some transactions go through the state (e.g. handgun sales only) and the remainder go through the federal NICS system, then the state is called a partial-POC state.

States that use the federal NICS system:

- Alabama
- Alaska
- American Samoa
- Arizona
- Arkansas

- Delaware
- D.C.
- Georgia
- Idaho
- Indiana
- Iowa
- Kansas
- Kentucky
- Louisiana
- Maine
- Massachusetts
- Michigan
- Minnesota
- Mississippi
- Missouri
- Montana
- New Mexico
- North Dakota
- N. Mariana Islands
- Ohio
- Oklahoma
- Puerto Rico

- Rhode Island
- South Carolina
- South Dakota
- Texas
- Vermont
- West Virginia
- Wyoming

Full-POC states:

- California
- Colorado
- Connecticut
- Hawaii
- Illinois
- Nevada
- New Jersey
- New York
- Oregon
- Pennsylvania
- Tennessee
- Utah
- Virginia

- Washington

Partial-POC states:

- Florida
- Maryland
- Nebraska
- New Hampshire
- North Carolina
- Wisconsin

For information on how to register with each system, how to use each system, and how much each system costs, please pursue more training ATF Firearm Compliance.

State-Specific Compliance

There are many states that have rules above and beyond the federal rules. For example, special forms must be filled out in Connecticut for handgun sales and California requires firearms to be on a specific approved roster.

Unfortunately, an attempt to list every state's requirements would be just as long as this entire book. Also, this book is to help you get your FFL and give you some education along the way - it does not, and can not, cover every possible facet of compliance.

Section Notes

Chapter 18 - Introduction

- Compliance is crucial
- Laws, rules, and regulations must all be followed

Chapter 19 - ATF Compliance

- It's all about "traceability"
- Most of ATF compliance is record-keeping
- Our ATF Compliance book is recommended
- Violations of the law are serious - willful violations equal loss of license or freedom
- GCA and NFA firearms are treated differently
- You may only conduct business on your licensed premises (except for gunshows and special events)
- You must maintain "reasonable" security
- Manufacturing over 50 firearms a year requires the payment of an excise tax
- Employees (W-2, not contractors) are an extension of your FFL

- Training, training, training!

Chapter 20 -U.S. Dept. of State/Dept. of Commerce Compliance

- There are two federal agencies that regulate exports: State and Commerce.
- The division of state that oversees its regulations and our industry is the (C) DDTC or Directorate of Defense Trade Controls and for Commerce, it is the BIS or Bureau of Industry and Security.
- The regulations created by State are the ITAR or International Traffic in Arms Regulations and the regulations created by Commerce are the EAR or Export Administration Regulations.
- Each of these regulations have a specific list of items that helps to determine how they are controlled. For State, the list is the USML or United Stated Munitions List and for Commerce it is the CCL or Commerce Control List.
- State regulates most firearms, their parts, ammo, and related info
- Commerce regulates shotguns with barrels greater than 18 inches, their parts, ammo, and related info.
- **An export is:**
    - sending or taking something out of the country,
    - disclosing "technical data" to a foreign person, OR
    - performing a "defense service" for a foreign person
- Technical data is any information that is NOT publicly available which can help someone make or operate a firearm. This includes drawings, specs, and special processes.
- A "defense service" is providing non- publicly available training to a foreign person.
- It is important to remember that an export can occur with technical data or a defense service even if it happens within our country!

- Here's the best advice I can give you in this area - be extremely careful with foreign persons. Except for a few exceptions, they can not possess firearms in this country and you can let them see or hear technical data!

- The last note here is that your employees MUST be trained - this protects you and them.

Chapter 21 -Record Keeping

- Many records to keep track of - a few listed in this book. You MUST learn more.
- Paper records are allowed
- Electronic records are highly recommended
- A&D Records are the heart of an FFL's records
- 4473 - Source of MOST violations for FFLs
- Multiple Sales Forms are easily forgotten and vary by state
- Many more forms (seemingly endless)

Chapter 23 -State-Level Compliance

- NICS vs POC States
- POC states can be full POC or only partial POC

INITIAL ATF INSPECTION

As part of the process to getting your FFL, you're going to have a visit from the ATF – this is considered your initial inspection.

This section covers what to expect and how to prepare.

Chapter 24

Preparing for ATF Visit

Step 1: Don't panic.

For some reason, soon-to-be FFLs start to panic during this period of waiting for their initial inspection. Don't. I believe that normal ATF compliance inspections are nothing to worry about and they are scarier than this initial inspection.

Most Industry Operations Investigators ("IOIs") are good people. Of book, as with all types of people, there are some jerks but you're not likely to encounter one. In fact, your biggest risk with an IOI is finding one that doesn't understand what is going on. I've encountered more than one IOI who wasn't a bad person but they seriously misunderstood firearm compliance and made things difficult until I could explain it to them (or I could explain it to their boss who explained it to them).

The initial inspection can last anywhere from one hour to a full day. It all depends on how prepared you are and how thorough the IOI wants to be.

Step 2: Educate yourself.

If you haven't gotten the hint yet, I'm trying to encourage you to get ATF compliance training. You likely have about 6-weeks until you're contacted by an IOI to schedule your initial inspection - don't regret not taking this time to learn as much as you can about firearm compliance. You'll make yourself more successful and you'll keep yourself out of trouble.

Also, when you're educated about the requirements, you'll make your initial inspection go much faster/easier and you'll start off on the right foot with the ATF. Trust me, I have IOIs that will actually ask me questions and learn from me during initial inspections.

They are trained to learn the regulations, but many of them don't have the real-world training and examples that you'll have if you study up before hand.

Step 3: Prepare your location.

You don't have to be completely ready to operate as an FFL, but you'd be wise to have a presentable area for the ATF. Think about security considerations. Think about a place for you and the ATF to sit and meet during your initial inspection. Also, make sure you don't have anything "questionable" laying around. The IOIs are not law enforcement, but they work with the ATF agents who are. Have your meeting place cleaned up and ready for your meeting.

Chapter 25

During ATF Inspection

Your job is to make it through the initial inspection and get your FFL. Your job is not to try to impress the ATF with your knowledge.

This advice applies to any time you are dealing with the ATF - there is such a thing as being too helpful. I have MANY clients who have wound up in trouble because they didn't know when to nod their head and say "yes, sir" or "yes, ma'am." For example, I've had a client who was asked by the ATF if there was ever a transaction that didn't feel right. The client thought about it and answered "well, you know, there was this one time where there was a weird guy..." Next thing you know, the client was charged with a serious violation of the Gun Control Act for proceeding with a transaction that they just admitted didn't "feel right."

Pay attention, take notes, and ask questions. The IOI is there to assess your professionalism and to help you succeed as an FFL. You will be given a stack of materials - ensure that the Youth Handgun Safety poster is included.

You will also be initialing up and down both sides of a form called the "Acknowledgement of Federal Firearms Regulations" (now completed as individual acknowledgments on a computer).

This is a VERY important form.

If you are non-compliant in the future, this is the form that the ATF is going to use against you by showing that you acknowledged that you were aware of your obligations. If you have questions as the IOI goes over this form - ask!

Also, if the IOI tells you something that doesn't sound correct, get it in writing. You still must follow the rules as they exist but if you followed the written advice of an ATF employee at least you can show that you weren't "willfully" violating the law.

RECEIPT OF FFL

When you get your FFL in the mail, you're not done.

This section covers what you need to do when you receive your FFL and your next steps.

NOTE: Unfortunately, you'll likely start getting spam texts/calls/emails before you actually get your paper copy of your FFL in the mail. It's annoying but it's often a great heads-up that your FFL is on its way. If you've already started your FFLSafe.com account, you'll be ready to be off and running once you have your FFL number.

Chapter 26

Day One With Your New FFL

In this chapter, we're going to cover:

- **Copies of Your New FFL**
- **Posting Documents**
- **Starting Your Business**

Copies of Your New FFL

The first thing you should do when you receive your new FFL in the mail is make a quality color copy/scan of your new license.

DO THIS BEFORE SIGNING YOUR FFL.

After you have a good scan/copy of your new and unsigned FFL, print out a copy, sign it, and then make a good scan/copy of the signed copy. You will then have the original paper FFL that you can file away and you will have two copies/scans: one unsigned and one signed.

When you need to send off a copy of your FFL for use, you can print an unsigned copy and then sign it as needed. Of book, you could just print out a pre-signed copy but technically, you should be signing a copy of your FFL for each use.

Posting Documents

Either use the original document or print out a signed copy of your FFL and post it on your wall in an obvious location. This is a legal requirement.

Also, post the Youth Handgun Safety poster that I encouraged you to get from the IOI during your initial inspection. This is also a legal requirement.

Starting Your Business

Many other compliance requirements now apply - e.g. keeping proper records, maintaining an A&D book, etc. Here's the last push for you to take the follow-on book in ATF Firearms Compliance.

Chapter 27

Resources

Federal Firearms Regulations Reference Guide

Paperback on Amazon: Federal Firearms Regulations Reference Guide: Firearm laws and ATF Rules and Regulations.[1]

Business Insurance

If you're considering insurance for your firearms business, I recommend reaching out to Lockton Affinity Outdoor. Of course, I cannot guarantee they will be able to provide you with coverage, but I use them for my FFL business and have been very satisfied. They cater to the firearms industry, so their team is very knowledgeable, and they work well with FFLs.

Wholesalers/Distributors

You're probably going to want to get set up with a distributor ASAP so that you can start ordering guns!

When making a new account with a distributor, be prepared to send a copy of your FFL and have your business information handy.

My favorite distributor to work with for home-based FFLs is Lipsey's. Just tell them RocketFFL sent you, and they'll set you up with an account! Here is their application to become a dealer with them: Lispsey's Application.

Banking

Now that you are a business with an FFL, you need a bank account.

If you're more comfortable with larger banks, they are an option, but many of them are anti-gun. In our experience, local banks or credit unions are the best resources for business checking accounts for firearms businesses.

1. Link available at the URL / QR Code in the Introduction Section

Make sure the bank account is set up as a business account in the name that you are using on your FFL.

Bookkeeping

I recommend starting now with a method of bookkeeping - if you don't have it set up now, you'll be playing catch-up later.

Many small businesses have great success with Quickbooks, but I recently switched to Xero and love it. You'll be fine with either.

Accounting

Unless you're financially savvy, you should also consider reaching out to and finding an accountant.

A good accountant's advice now is way better than the best accountant's advice after a year has passed.

Chapter 28

Accepting Credit Cards

If you're going to be selling guns, accepting credit cards is effectively a necessity.

Sure, you can run your FFL without credit cards, however, they are extremely popular for in-person customers and required for almost all online transactions.

Unfortunately, accepting credit cards is not that simple.

We're going to walk you through how to accept credit cards for just online/web orders, and also how to accept them from in-person customers. For online-only sales, you'll just need to set up some accounts. However, for in-person transactions, you'll need a card reader at a minimum and perhaps a full Point of Sale (POS) system.

Firearm Sales and Credit Cards

For online sales, the three biggest credit card processors that work with most e-commerce stores are Stripe, Square, and PayPal. Unfortunately, none of them allow firearm sales.

For example, here's the language that bans firearm sales from the three most popular online credit card solutions:

PayPal: "You may not use the PayPal service for activities that... relate to transactions involving... ammunition, firearms, or certain firearm parts or accessories..." (PayPal terms)

Square: "Prohibited Goods and Services... Sales of (i) firearms, firearm parts or hardware, and ammunition; or (ii) weapons..." (Square terms)

Stripe: "The following categories of businesses and business practices are prohibited from using the Stripe Service... Regulated Products and Services:...age-restricted goods or services, weapons, and munitions..." (Stripe terms)

These big three won't open a firearm merchant account because they consider certain industries too "high risk." There are some companies that will open up a high-risk merchant account, but the costs are typically too high to make sense for most firearms retailers.

Now for the good news: Just because these merchant services don't allow you to accept a payment for a gun sale doesn't mean you're out of luck with credit card processing.

You can still accept credit card payments as a gun dealer as long as you set up your merchant account with a gun-friendly credit card processor through a system like FFLS afe.com

Understanding Credit Card Payments

Signing up through FFLSafe.com is the first step of accepting credit cards for firearms sales for your business after you have your FFL license.

But, there are a few more steps that will follow before you can process a credit card transaction for your gun shop.

Let's explore some of the terms and topics that gun retailers will need to understand:

Payment Processor The payment processor is the company that actually processes the credit card transaction. This company is sometimes referred to as a merchant account provider and they offer payment solutions as a service.

This is the company that actually provides retail firearms merchant accounts. We recommend checking out Payroc as your payment processor to help you set up your merchant account.

But, unfortunately, accepting credit cards can be a bit complicated and they aren't the only company you'll need to have an account with.

Payment Gateway Firearms merchants will also need a payment gateway to accept credit cards. The gateway is the company that handles the transaction through your eCommerce platform or in-store POS system. They are the bridge (or gateway) between your customer's credit card and the payment processor (merchant account).

The biggest payment gateway is Authorize.net but there are more affordable and smaller options available. If you go with Payroc, they'll help you set up the right option for you.

Financial Institution (Bank) Firearm retailers will, of book, need a bank. You will need to make sure that your bank allows business accounts for gun merchants.

The gateway gathers the credit card details for the transaction, and the payment processor runs the credit card and receives the money and then deposits the money you earned into your financial institution.

Chargeback A chargeback is when a customer files a dispute with their credit card company about the transaction - typically because of fraud, unauthorized transactions, or failure to refund money.

These are obviously not good for you.

To avoid excessive chargebacks on your merchant account you should document transactions well and explain any terms and conditions clearly. If you get a chargeback, you'll have a chance to dispute it and respond with details showing that it was a legitimate transaction.

Simple tips here are having good tracking details for shipments and gathering plenty of details about your customers. Being vigilant not only helps protect you and your business, it will also help protect people who had their credit card numbers stolen and used by a criminal with you.

Ecommerce Making sales in your gun shop is great, but to be competitive in this market, you'll need to strongly consider online sales (eCommerce).

You can either set up your own website with an eCommerce system, use an online store-in-a-box system like the Ammoready platform, or you can sell on online auction sites like GunBroker.

Whichever eCommerce system you choose, you will need to have a payment processor as part of your payment process.

PCI Compliance This is a confusing term for many gun dealers. To accept credit cards, you need to comply with federal laws and help to ensure that you are properly protecting your customers' credit card information.

PCI compliance refers to following all of these rules. After you sign up with Payroc, they'll help walk you through the process to ensure that you are PCI compliant.

If you don't have this set up within the first few months of accepting credit cards, you can be charged a non-compliance fee.

How to Start Accepting Credit Cards for Firearms Sales

Unfortunately, federal firearms laws aren't the only thing you need to worry about to run your business. You now need to know about, and comply with federal laws related to credit card payments (see Electronic Fund Transfer Act).

Don't panic! They aren't that hard to learn and follow - and we're going to walk you through each step of your payment processing solution.

Step 1 - Sign up With a Payment Processor. Once you have your FFL and are ready to be a gun store, your business will need to be able to start accepting credit cards. Signing up through FFLSafe.com is as simple as I could make it.

Step 2 - Set up Bank and Payment Gateway. Choose a bank that will work with a firearms dealer and select the payment gateway that is recommended by your payment processor - this will ensure that you select one that works with your merchant account and also that you select the right one for your needs (smaller ones are free while large ones charge a monthly fee).

Step 3 - Set up Your Ecommerce Platform. Depending on what is right for your firearm business, set up your eCommerce platform and connect it to your payment gateway.

Step 4 - Ensure PCI Compliance. Follow the instructions from your Payment processor to make sure you are compliant with the privacy rules.

Merchant Account Summary

Gun merchants have a few steps to go through in order to accept credit cards for firearms sales.

But, if you go through FFLSafe.com, you'll be helped through each step of the process.

BECOMING AN SOT

After you have your FFL, you may want to become a Special Occupational Taxpayer (SOT) so that you can work with National Firearms Act (NFA) firearms like silencers, machine guns, and more.

This section of this book will walk you through the requirements to become an SOT and how to register as one.

Chapter 29

SOT Background

In this chapter, we're going to cover:

- **Special Occupational Taxpayer System**
- **Categories of firearms**
- **NFA Firearm Tracking**

Special Occupational Taxpayer system

The National Firearms Act of 1934 (NFA) was enacted in response to the gang crime of the era and an attempted Presidential assassination. The NFA required federal registration and taxation of certain firearms. These particular firearms, referred to as "NFA firearms" are a special class of firearms that Congress determined to be especially dangerous or likely to be used in the era's gang related crimes. At this time, the ATF was part of the Treasury Department - thus the regulation of firearms via a tax. The ATF didn't move to the Department of Justice until much later.

NFA firearms are Silencers (suppressors), Short Barreled Rifles (SBRs), Short Barreled Shotguns (SBSs), Any Other Weapons (AOWs), and machine guns (full-auto). These are the only firearms that are tracked in a federal database.

Contrary to popular belief, standard firearm transactions and possession are not tracked in a database (or, at least, they're not supposed to be). The tax imposed on these firearms in 1934 was $200. Much later, the tax for AOWs was reduced to $5 and, as of 2026, the tax on Silencers, SBRs, SBSs, and AOWs has been reduced to $0.

Previously, an FFL would become a Special Occupational Taxpayer (SOT) so that they could pay the tax once a year ($500 in most cases) instead of per NFA firearm (used to be

$200 in most cases). With the tax being reduced to $0 for most NFA firearms, however, you might be wonder why you'd want to register as an SOT. Well, it isn't just a tax saving option - it is required for FFLs to manufacture NFA firearms and for dealers to take advantage of some benefits in dealing in NFA firearms.

The cost of registering as an SOT varies depending on the class of SOT (next chapter).

Categories of Firearms

There are two main categories of firearms. The first category of firearms are "standard" firearms which are covered by the Gun Control Act of 1968 (GCA). The second category of firearms, which have stricter controls, are covered by the National Firearms Act of 1934 (NFA). Although the GCA was passed 34 years after the NFA, the GCA is considered "Title I" of federal firearms laws and the NFA is considered "Title II."

Examples of GCA / Title I firearms are: shotguns, rifles, and handguns.

Examples of NFA / Title II firearms are: silencers (suppressors), short barrel rifles and shotguns, and machine guns (full-auto). These are discussed more in Chapter 35 - NFA Firearms.

NFA Firearm Tracking

Many people don't know that the ATF is not allowed to keep a database of what firearms are owned by whom. This restriction, however, only applies to standard/Title I/GCA firearms. NFA Firearms, on the other hand, are tracked in an ATF database. This record maintained by the ATF is called the National Firearms Registry and Transfer Record (NFR&TR).

When an NFA firearm is made or imported, it is entered into the NFR&TR. Each time the firearm is transferred, the ATF processes the transfer and, if approved, the NFA firearm is then tracked as being possessed by the new recipient.

As part of an ATF compliance inspection, the ATF will likely show up with a copy of your log from the NFR&TR to confirm that you have only the NFA firearms that you should have. Transfers are covered in Chapter 35.

Also, there is very likely to be a discrepancy with your actual NFA firearm inventory and the ATF's NFR&TR. In fact, whenever this has been an issue for an FFL, I've never seen the ATF's NFR&TR be accurate. Your records must be perfect or you'll be in trouble - their records never seem to be.

Chapter 30

Classes of SOT

In this chapter, we're going to cover:

- **Classes of SOTs**
- **Choosing Which Class of SOT to Become**
- **SOT Cost**

Classes of SOT

In order to deal, manufacture, or import NFA /Title II firearms, the FFL holder must also become a Special Occupational Taxpayer (SOT).

Different classes of SOTs may engage in different activities.

- Class 1 SOT – These SOTs may Import and deal NFA / Title II firearms
- Class 2 SOT – These SOTs may manufacture and deal NFA / Title II firearms
- Class 3 SOT – These SOTs may deal NFA / Title II firearms

Here's a good time to address some terminology that is very often mis-used in our industry. A Federal Firearm License (FFL) is something you have while a Special Occupational Taxpayer (SOT) is something that you are.

You don't get an "FFL and SOT."

You get an FFL and *become* an SOT.

Also, you might hear people talk about "class 3 firearms." "Class 3" is NOT a type of firearm. "Class 3" is a type of SOT an FFL holder is to deal in NFA firearms. An FFL holder can also be a "Class 1" or "Class 2" SOT depending on whether they import and deal or manufacturer and deal NFA / Title II firearms.

Choosing Which Class of SOT to Become

Your choice of which class of SOT to become is dependent largely on which type of FFL you have (which was chosen based on the type of firearms activity you wanted to engage in).

See the table below for a simplified breakdown of which class of SOT is needed for each FFL. In the "FFL" column you'll see each type of FFL. In the "purpose" column you'll see what that FFL, by itself, allows. In the "NFA /Title II" columns you'll see what other activities that FFL holder may engage in if they are also a particular class of SOT. AP stands for Armor Piercing Ammunition and DD stands for Destructive Device.

As a note, being an SOT is an option for all FFL holders but FFL types 9, 10 and 11. As you can see in the table, these are the three FFLs which allow SOTs to work with Armor Piercing Ammunition and Destructive Devices. These FFL holders are required to also be SOTs.

For example, with just a Type 7 FFL, you are only allowed to manufacture and deal GCA / Title I firearms. By also becoming an SOT, then you may manufacture and deal NFA / Title II firearms except for Armor Piercing Ammunition and Destructive Devices. If you also want to work with those, then you'll need to get a Type 10 FFL.

		NFA / Title II (must be SOT)					
FFL	Purpose	Deal	Manufacture	Import	SOT Class	AP	DD
Type 1	Dealer or Gunsmith of Title I (GCA) firearms	✓	✗	✗	3	✗	✗
Type 2	Pawnbroker dealing Title I (GCA) firearms	✓	✗	✗	3	✗	✗
Type 3	Curio and Relic Collector	✗	✗	✗	-	✗	✗
Type 6	Manufacturer of Ammunition	✗	✗	✗	-	✗	✗
Type 7	Manufacturer/Dealer of Title I (GCA) firearms	✓	✓	✗	2	✗	✗
Type 8	Importer/Dealer of Title I (GCA) firearms and ammunition	✓	✗	✓	1	✗	✗
Type 9	Dealer of Title 1 (GCA) firearms	✓	✗	✗	3	✓	✓
Type 10	Manufacturer/Dealer of Title I (GCA) firearms	✓	✓	✗	2	✓	✓
Type 11	Importer/Dealer of Title I (GCA) firearms	✓	✗	✓	1	✓	✓

Classes of SOT

SOT Cost

To become an SOT you're going to pay at least $500 per year or, at most, $1,000 per year. The difference in cost depends on the type of FFL you have and the amount of sales you make within a given year.

The SOT registration periods runs from July 1st of one year to June 30th of the next year. This means that your registration as an SOT expires on June 30th, regardless of when you registered.

Depending on when you start your business, this can mean that you'll either need to wait until July 1 to start working with NFA firearms or you might have to pay for a full first year's registration even though June 30th might be less than a year away.

If you're starting business on June 15th, it's probably wise to register as an SOT starting July 1 and wait a couple of weeks to start working with NFA firearms. If you don't wait, you'll be paying a full year's tax for only two weeks of business and you'll be paying again for activity on July 1.

To wait or not is your decision.

	FFL			SOT		
FFL	Application Fee	Renewal Fee	Duration (years)	Tax-Rate (under $500k yearly sales)	Tax-Rate (over $500k yearly sales)	Duration (years)
Type 1	$200	$90	3	$500	$500	1
Type 2	$200	$90	3	$500	$500	1
Type 3	$30	$30	3	n/a	n/a	1
Type 6	$30	$30	3	$500	$1000	1
Type 7	$150	$150	3	$500	$1000	1
Type 8	$150	$150	3	$500	$1000	1
Type 9	$3000	$3000	3	$500	$1000	1
Type 10	$3000	$3000	3	$500	$1000	1
Type 11	$3000	$3000	3	$500	$1000	1

Chapter 31

Taxpayer Requirements

In this chapter, we're going to cover:

- **Taxpayer Identity**
- **Necessity for an EIN**
- **Different Locations for Business**
- **Separate Location for Storage**
- **Employee Considerations**

Taxpayer Identity

Remember, an SOT is something that you become, not something that you have. Many people think that an SOT is an upgrade of sorts for your FFL - this isn't technically true – it is an upgrade for you/your business as a taxpayer. You, as an SOT, may have as many FFLs as you want/need at a location and your registration as an SOT applies to all of your FFLs and locations because you are the SOT, not the actual FFL.

Of course, a certain Class of SOT is still needed for each particular FFL. Therefore, if you are a Class 3 SOT as a Dealer (Type 1 FFL), and you choose to also get a Type 7 Manufacturer's FFL because you want to manufacture NFA firearms, then you'll need to also become a Class 2 SOT. This isn't technically an upgrade for your Type 7 FFL but you need to be a Class 2 SOT in order to manufacture NFA firearms. As a Class 3 SOT with a Type 1 Dealer's FFL, you can get a Type 7 FFL without registering as a Class 2 SOT if you don't manufacture NFA firearms.

Because you are the SOT, your registration is for your business (whether as an individual or an actual formed business) and the ATF recognizes you by your Employer Identification Number (EIN). Your SOT registration paperwork will arrive with only your business information on it - not any information about whichever FFLs you may have.

Why does this matter?

First, it saves you from worrying about re-registering as an SOT if you have a Type 1 FFL and you want to get a second Type 1 FFL.

Second, it makes it MUCH easier to move NFA firearms from one of your licenses to another (even at another location). See Chapter 35 for more on this.

This is important when you are setting up your business, especially if you plan to have multiple FFLs or locations. By keeping everything under the same business (EIN), you are the same SOT in the eyes of the ATF. By making different locations different businesses, however, it might be a better decision in certain instances when you're concerned about liability, tax issues, ownership, or selling parts of your business. However, you'll have to transfer NFA firearms between these different business just as you would if you sold it to an unrelated business. This is a decision that you should make with your business-planning attorney.

EIN Needed

You must have an Employee Identification Number (EIN) in order to register as an SOT.

This is true even if you are operating as a sole proprietor (which I strongly discourage). You may use your Social Security Number as a sole proprietor for most purposes but in this case, you need to get an EIN.

Different Locations for Business

Despite what you just learned about your SOT status being recognized by EIN and not your FFLs or locations, each location must be registered and you must pay the tax for each location. Thank government bureaucracy for this illogical situation.

If you have a different location from which you wish to engage in business with firearms, you'll need a unique FFL at that location and that location will need to be listed on, or added to, your SOT registration and you'll have to pay the appropriate tax amount for each location, even though it is the same entity making the SOT registration (just at a different location).

Therefore, one location with multiple FFLs = one SOT registration and payment.

Multiple locations as the same company = adding each location to your SOT registration and paying for each location. Multiple locations with different companies/EINs (may happen depending on your business structure) = unique FFLs and unique SOT registrations and payments for each company.

As a note, a transfer of an NFA firearm to different locations but within the same company isn't really an "NFA transfer." We'll cover this more later.

Separate Location for Storage

Note, I specifically wrote above that you'll need a separate SOT registration and a unique FFL for a separate location in which "you wish to engage in business with firearms."

If you have a separate location for the storage of firearms ONLY, then you do not need an FFL nor do you need to list that location on your SOT registration. There's a special way to handle this, not only for setting it up but also for proper record keeping.

Employees

Once an NFA firearm is properly registered to your business, whether it was transferred to you on a Form 3 from another FFL or whether you manufactured it on a Form 2 (don't worry, we'll cover these later), then your company is allowed to possess that NFA firearm.

NOTE - I used the word "possess" and not "own." As a general rule, the ATF doesn't care about who owns a firearm, they care about who possess it. For example, if a customer sends you a firearm for repair, they still own it but you need to have it properly acquired so that you are allowed to posses it. Likewise, if you lend a firearm to a customer to take on a hunting trip, it doesn't matter that your business still owns the firearm, a proper transfer will need to take place before the customer may possess it.

When your company is the proper possessor of an NFA firearm (or any firearm for that matter), any one of your actual employees may possess it in connection with their role as an employee. This is because actual employees are acting as the business when they are doing business activities. After all, the company is just something on paper - it can't posses anything.

This means that an actual employee may take an NFA firearm off-site to demonstrate it for sale or perform testing at a range.

It is vitally important that all five of these things are true in order for this to be legal:

1. The NFA firearm is properly acquired by your company

2. The employee is an actual employee ("bona fide" is the term commonly used)

3. The use is an actual and legitimate (again, "bona fide") business purpose

4. Local laws are followed by the employee (no walking around Times Square with a machine gun!)

5. The firearm is properly logged out of your records for this temporary use (this is called a "temporary assignment" and is NOT a "disposition" in your A&D records).

What is a bona fide employee?

A bona fide employee is hired and paid by your company on a W-2

It is NOT a contractor paid on a 1099

What is a bona fide business use?

e.g. sales demos, photo shoots, testing, etc.

It is a use that has a direct company benefit and is directed by the company

I have seen ATF violations for employees taking firearms on a hunting trip. There are ways to protect yourself in these situations and to allow a wide range of activities for Temporary Assignments.

It is NOT going to the range just for fun or keeping it at home because it's "cool."

Chapter 32

SOT Registration

In this lesson, we're going to cover:

- **Methods of filling out the SOT Registration**
- **SOT Registration Process**
- **SOT Application Steps**
- **Application Checklist and Submisison**

Application Process

The registration process itself is even simpler than the FFL application process. To become an SOT, you will complete it on paper by sending one packet to the ATF and you will keep a copy for your records or you can now complete it fully online using the ATF's eForm system.

I'll walk you through how to fill out the registration form.

Don't worry about each step now – I'm including the information below to give you an idea of what we're going to cover. By the time you're done with this Chapter, your registration form will be complete and I'll provide you a simple checklist (not that you'll need it) to use to make sure you're ready to go!

You may complete this process electronically, on paper by-hand, or a bit of both.

- If you are computer-savvy, and would like to register electronically and completely online, you can use the ATF's eForm system.[1]

- If you'd like to fill out the application as a pdf on your computer but you'd rather print it out, sign it by hand, and mail it in, I have included a fillable .pdf of the necessary form on the extra resources page for this book at the URL / QR code in the Introduction of this book.

- If you're old-school and would rather hold the materials in your hands, you can either print out the form I've provided or you can order one from the ATF and you can fill out the entire form by hand.

SOT Registration Process

1. Obtain an Employee Identification Number from the IRS.

If you complete this process online, you will be able to obtain your EIN immediately after completing the application online with the IRS.[2]

2. Obtain an FFL.

It's likely that you already have an FFL or, at least, you've already applied for one. You must have a valid FFL before you can submit your SOT registration.

3. Complete Special Tax Registration and Return National Firearms Act form (ATF Form 5630.7)

This can be done entirely online using eForms or you can fill out the application to mail in.

4. Pay the SOT tax.

You can either do this as part of your eForm process or, if you're mailing in your application, you can draft a check payable to "Bureau of Alcohol, Tobacco, Firearms and Explosives" for dollar amount of your chosen SOT Class and yearly sales revenue amount. As a note, include your EIN on the check.

5. Submit your registrion.

---

1. Link to the ATF's eForm system is available by following the URL / QR code in the Introduction section of this book.

2. Link to the IRS EIN application is available by following the URL / QR code in the Introduction section of this book.

You do this by either finalizing the online process or by sending the SOT registration form and check to the ATF.

6. Wait for ATF to process registration and issue you a Special Tax Stamp (ATF Form 5630.6A) for each location.

SOT Application Steps

Your SOT registration may be filled out in a few different ways:

By Hand: You may fill out a paper version of the registration by:

- Ordering a copy from the ATF, or
- Downloading and printing a PDF of the registration (on white paper)

Electronically: If you prefer to fill out the application electronically, however, you may:

- Open the .pdf of the registration form, fill it out on your computer screen, and then print it (on white paper), or
- Fill out the entire registration online using the ATF's eForm system

I am including instructions below to fill out the actual registration form by hand (or via the fillable pdf) and also instructions on how to use eForms to complete an SOT registration.

INSTRUCTIONS FOR FILLING OUT SOT REGISTRATION FORM:

Please see below for notes for each question on the registration form. If you are filling out the registration form directly (either by-hand or electronically), I suggest you follow along with each number.

As a general rule, I don't like to leave spaces on forms blank – if you don't have relevant information for any particular section, please write "n/a."

I have included a sample form at the URL / QR code in the introduction section as an example own how the application should be filled out.

STEP 1. Fill out SOT Registration Form.

STEP 2. Print out your application (if you filled out the pdf electronically).

STEP 3. Sign, include your title in your business, and date in boxes 21, 22, and 23.

STEP 4. Make a copy (photocopy or scan) of the complete form.

This copy is for your records. You should start a file now to keep all documents and correspondence with the ATF – your FFL application should have been the first thing in this file.

NOTES for Each Question on the Form - PLEASE FOLLOW ALONG

Circle the applicable option: "a" if this is your first time registering as an SOT, "b" if you are renewing your SOT status, "c" if you are amending your SOT registration (for changes not including location or SOT Class) or, "d" if you are registering a change to your location or SOT Class.

Employer Identification Number (EIN). If you don't have this yet, stop here and go obtain one HERE. If you insist on starting your registration without an EIN, the ATF will issue you a temporary identification number to start processing your registration. However, you won't get your tax stamp issued until you have your EIN and you risk delays due to mixups of your temporary and actual numbers.

Tax Period Covering. Enter the date you want the registration to start and the date of the nearest June 30th. For example, if you fill this out on June 20th of one year, then that same year must be used for the year after June 30th.

FFL Number. Use your main FFL number here. Include each additional FFL number that you want to be covered by this SOT registration on a separate piece of paper showing your name, trade name, address and employer identification number.

Name or Corporation. You should enter the actual name that exists on your FFL.

Trade Name. If you used a trade name on your FFL, you should enter the same information here.

Business Address. This must match the business address on your FFL. This is the address of the licensed premises – it is where the ATF expects to find you conducting your business. This can not be a P.O. Box. As we already covered, you may have an off-site storage location for firearms – do not include that address here.

Business Address City, State, and Zip Code. Continues from previous.

Mailing Address. If you want mail delivered to an address other than your actual location, you may include that here. This address may be a P.O. Box.

Mailing Address City, State, and Zip Code. Continued from previous.

Business Telephone Number. Enter a number where the ATF can reach you during normal business hours. This should match the business number you provided on your FFL application.

E-mail address: Enter your main company email address.

Tax Computation. Calculate the tax owed by multiplying the number of locations for which you want to be registered as each Class of SOT. If your sales are, or will be, less than $500,000 (for all sales, not just firearms sales) then you qualify for the "reduced rate."

For example, if you will be under the sales amount and you want to be a Class 3 SOT as a Type 1 Dealer FFL with one location, then you'll pay $500. If you want two locations, it'll be $1,000. If you're over the sales amount threshold, then it'll be $1,000 per location.

Total Tax Due. Enter the calculated amount from #13 here.

Ownership Information. Select whichever applies. If you are an LLC, select "Other" and write-in "LLC"

Ownership Responsibility. Enter each "Responsible Person" from your FFLs here. List additional names on separate piece of paper showing your name, trade name, address and employer identification number. (this can be the same piece of paper used for #4)

Gross Receipts Less Than $500,000. If you qualified for the reduced rate from #13, then select this box.

Existing Business With a Change In: If you've previously registered this business as an SOT, select this box and only select the appropriate boxes for any information that may have changed and needs updated from your prior registration. If nothing has changed, select the box for #18, skip the boxes with each category of information and skip #19.

Discontinued Business. If you are ceasing business operations, select this box.

Date: If a "discontinued business," enter the date your business operations ceased.

Signature. This form must be signed by the individual owner, a partner, or, in the case of a corporation, by an individual authorized to sign for the corporation.

Title. Enter the business title for the person who signed in #21.

Date. Enter the date the form was signed.

INSTRUCTIONS FOR USING eFORMS FOR YOUR SOT REGISTRATION:

If you choose to use eForms to complete your registration, you will have skipped the instructions above and, instead, use these instructions:

STEP 1. Register for ATF eForms.

STEP 2. Complete ATF Form 5630.7 - Special Tax Registration and Return - National Firearms Act.

STEP 3. Pay your registration tax on Pay.gov.

STEP 1 – Registering for ATF eForms: If you do not yet have an eForms account, you will need to create one.

1. First, navigate to the ATF eForms Website. It should look like the image below.

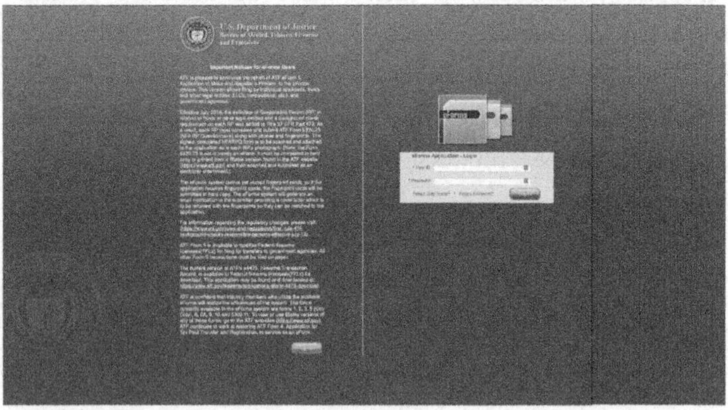

2. Select "REGISTER" by clicking on the green [Register] button.
3. Fill in Contact Details.

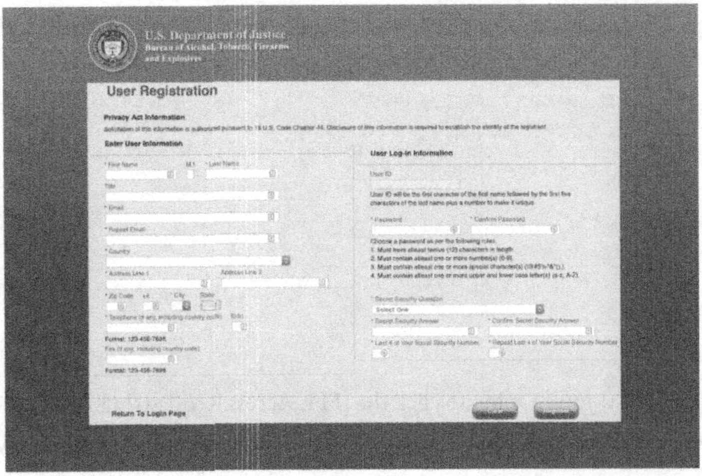

On this page you'll enter the user information and contact details.

This is for your account personally as a user – this is NOT for your FFL information.

Once you fill in your name, you should see that your username is automatically filled in for you.

Once you have entered all of the information, please make sure that you have your username and password saved before you click on [Register] at the bottom right.

4. Sign in to eForms

You should have been kicked out of the registration process and the eForms system will require you to sign back in.

Sign in to eForms using the username and password you just created and saved.

5. Associate User ID to Your FFL

Now that you have an eForms account for you as an individual (remember, in Step 3 I mentioned that you're setting this up for you and not your FFL), you are going to need to add your FFL so that the ATF understands that you are a user that will be filing forms for the FFL.

NOTE: You can manage more than one FFL from your same user account – you'll just have to associate each FFL by following the instructions below.

Click on the [My Profile] tab

Click the [FFL/AECA/EIN Access] tab

Click on the [Request Access] button

After these three steps, you should see a section titled: Request FFL/AECA/EIN Access

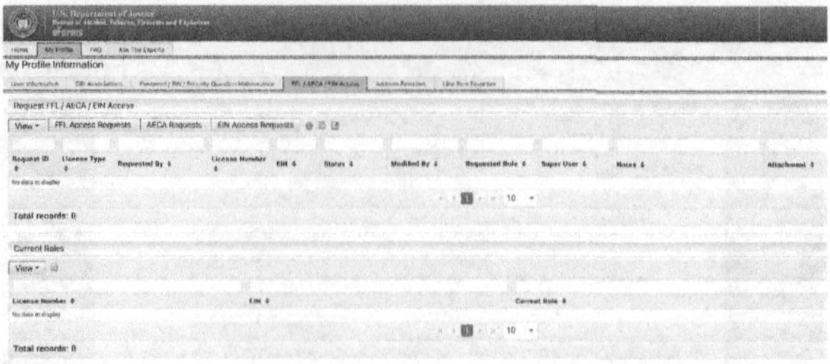

In this window, you're going to click the [FFL Access Requests] tab.

A new window will pop-up where you can enter the first 3 and last 5 digits of your FFL number.

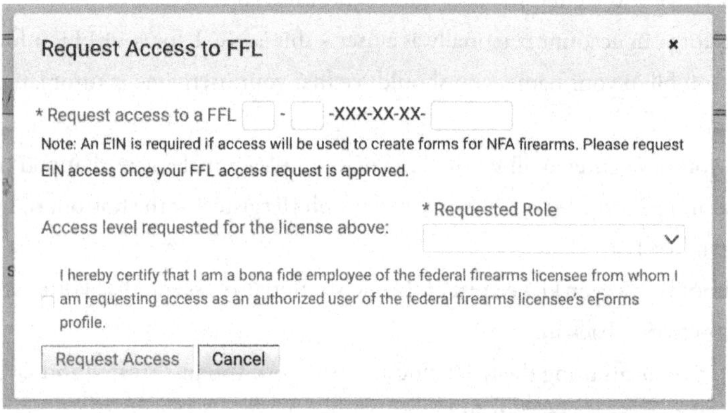

You're going to have to select a User Role for your account on this FFL.

If you are the main representative of your FFL, then you'll select "Super User.'

NOTE: Each FFL needs at least one Super User.

If, however, you are an employee of the FFL that will be filling our forms and are not the main representative, then you should select "Submitter."

If you selected "Super User," then you'll receive an email confirming your request and it will be a few days until the ATF approves you as a Super User.

Once your account has been associated with an FFL, the FFL will appear in your list of FFLs in the system

STEP 2 – Complete ATF Form 5630.7

From the main dashboard in your eForms account, select the form 5630.7.

Upon selecting the form, you should see the option to pay your SOT registration for the first time or to renew.

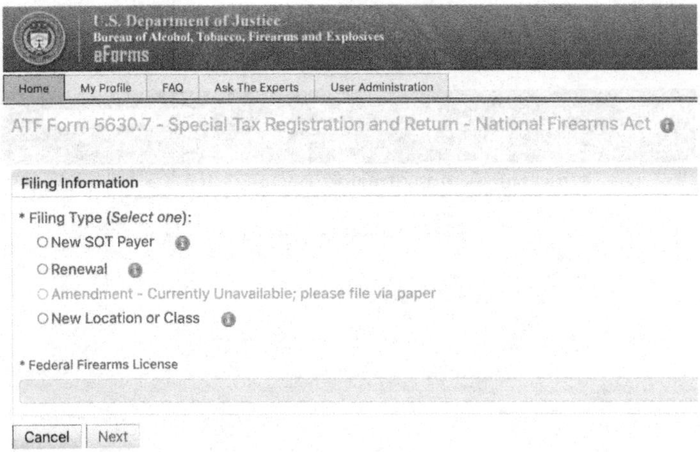

Select "New SOT Payer," select your FFL which should appear in the dropdown, and then click on [Next]. If your FFL does not appear yet, you might need to wait until the ATF associates it with your account.

You will be walked through the process for your new registration which involves confirming some of the information already on file for your FFL and entering new information if it is not already there like your EIN.

During the process, you will be making your SOT Class and tax election. If you have gross receipts for the business of less than $500,000, be sure to select that check-box at the top left so that the amounts for each class show the lowered rates.

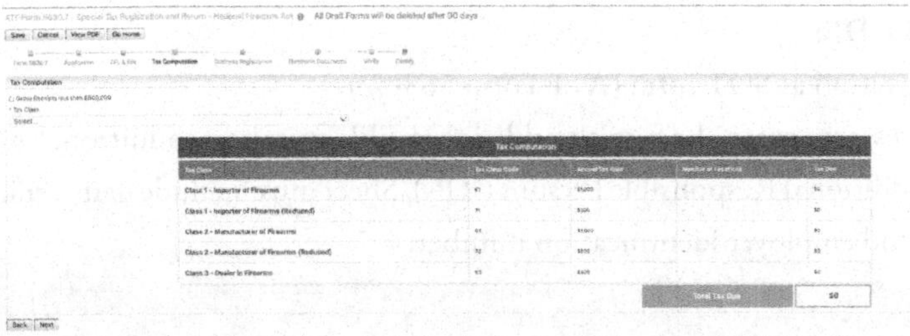

Select the class and rate that is appropriate for your FFL and continue.

You'll be adding yourself as the business owner, verifying, and then certifying your information.

STEP 3 – Pay Your Registration Tax on Pay.gov

Use Pay.gov to pay your SOT registration tax by navigating to the page on Pay.gov for the Form 5630.7[3]

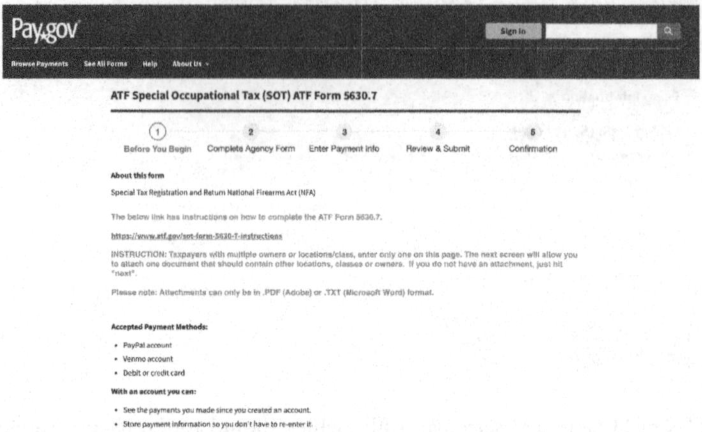

Application Checklist and Submission

If you're mailing in your registration, the following is just your checklist to ensure that you have everything you need. If you completed the registration via eForms, you may skip this part.

Packet to ATF

INCLUDE:

Registration as SOT form (ATF Form 5630.7)

If necessary, extra sheet with additional FFL numbers, additional locations, and/or additional Responsible Persons (RPs). Sheet must include name, trade name, address and employer identification number.

---

3. Link to the Pay.gov page for the 5630.7 is available by following the URL / QR code in the Introduction section of this book.

Check for amount in box #14 from SOT Registration form made out to "Bureau of Alcohol, Tobacco, Firearms and Explosives" with EIN on the check.

Application Submission

Now that your registration materials are complete, it's time to put them in the mail. Send your packet and your envelope to the ATF at the below address.

Packet to ATF:

MAIL TO:

Special Occupational Tax (SOT) – NFA

P.O. Box 6200-13

Portland, OR 97228-6200

You're Done!

Once your materials are in the mail, or you completed the process on eForms, you have now officially completed your SOT registration!

Congratulations!

After this step, you're done for a few weeks and you get to wait on the ATF to process your paperwork.

While you're waiting, it's a great time to start learning about all of the requirements you just signed up for. The next chapter introduces some of the NFA firearms compliance areas that you need to be aware of.

Chapter 33

NFA Compliance

In this lesson, we're going to cover:

- **NFA Firearms**
- **State Compliance and Traveling with NFA Firearms**
- **NFA Transfers Generally**
- **Transfers to Same EIN**
- **NFA Forms**

NFA Firearms

NFA Firearms, or Title II firearms, are a specially regulated class of firearms. The following categories are all considered "NFA Firearms."

Please keep in mind that there is much more about the nuances of these firearms and how they must be handled/treated which is covered in our ATF Compliance program.

Remember, this is a course on how to become an SOT with a bunch of extra info I've included to help you understand what is going on in the NFA world. I believe that this extra information is what makes these guides the best available. However, I can only include so much in a course on Becoming an SOT. The follow-on program on ATF Compliance is designed to help you operate once you've got your FFL and become an SOT.

Please don't rely on this BRIEF overview alone when it comes to making decisions about NFA firearms. You must be very careful to know what you're dealing with. I've had more than one client who received a firearm as a standard firearm which turned out to be an NFA firearm (mostly Machine Guns and SBRs) upon closer inspection.

Silencers

It is very popular to call these "suppressors." I use the term "silencer" because that is the word the ATF uses, it is the word used in the laws, rules, and regulations, and it is the word used by the inventor of them, Hiram Maxim.

Yes, I've included silencers in the category "NFA Firearms" because technically, silencers are considered to be "firearms" under federal law. Go figure. The very basic federal legal definition of a firearm includes any weapon which shoots a projectile by the force of an explosive. Therefore, potato guns that use hairspray are firearms whereas potato guns that use compressed air are not firearms because there's no explosion. Be careful, some states treat air guns as firearms.

The rest of the federal definition of a firearm includes the frame/receiver of a firearm, anything that can be "readily converted" to be a frame/receiver or complete firearm, silencers, and destructive devices. This definition comes from the Gun Control Act of 1968 (GCA) which means that silencers are in both the National Firearms Act of 1934 and the GCA.

Not only are complete silencers considered firearms, but also EVERY PART of a silencer is also considered to be a silencer. This is very different from standard firearms where the only part that is a firearm is the frame/receiver. Therefore, a silencer baffle, by itself, is a silencer. However, not all of the parts need to be marked nor registered/controlled as a complete silencer.

Machine Guns/ Full-Auto

Machine Guns / Full Auto firearms are firearms which expel more than one projectile by a single pull of the trigger. Machine Guns made before 1986 can be transferred to non-FFLs (customers) whereas Machine Guns made after 1986 can only be transferred to government entities or FFLs who have proof that the transfer is intended to be used for a government entity. These are called "non-transferrable" Machine Guns because the can't be transferred to normal folks.

Shotguns, even though more than one projectile can come out, are not necessarily Machine Guns. Of course, there can be a Machine Gun / Full Auto shotgun, but a single shotgun shell doesn't count. Likewise devices to give a Full Auto-like effect aren't necessarily Machine Guns. For example slide-fire stocks still require a pull of the trigger for every bullet. Also, special triggers that fire on pull and release aren't Machine Guns because only one bullet comes out when the trigger is pulled.

Certain parts designed to convert a firearm to Full Auto are also machine guns. Examples include Full Auto sears.

Short Barreled Rifles (SBRs)

These are rifles which have a barrel under 16 inches in length or an overall length of less than 26 inches. There are plenty of extra things to learn here like how to properly measure a barrel's length, how the SBRs must be marked, and so on.

Short Barrel Shotguns (SBSs)

These are shotguns which have a barrel under 18 inches in length or an overall length of less than 26 inches.

Any Other Weapons (AOWs)

This is a complicated class of NFA firearms (yes, they really made a class of firearm called "Any Other"). This category includes disguised firearms (cane guns, pen guns, etc.), pistols with a foregrip, pistols designed to fire a shotgun shell with a smooth barrel, and more. For a bit more info, feel free to read my article that I wrote for Mossberg about one of their products, Would a Shotgun By Any Other Name Still Be a Shotgun?

Destructive Devices

These are firearms that have a bore diameter greater than .5 inches (over 50 cal) and any explosive, incendiary, or poison gas, (A) bomb, (B) grenade, (C) rocket having a propellant charge of more than 4 ounces, (D) missile having an explosive charge of more than 1/4 ounce, (E) mine or (F) similar device.

I assume that the only Destructive Device that you'll have to worry about are firearms over 50 cal. Each of these firearms can be treated as a normal firearm (non-NFA) if it has been exempted by the ATF for a sporting purpose. Therefore, 12 gauge shotguns aren't Destructive Devices because they've been exempted.

State Compliance and Traveling with NFA Firearms.

Sorry to keep doing this to you but this is another area that has WAY too much to cover in a section of a book on how to Become an SOT.

For now, I'll tell you this: Be very careful when traveling with NFA firearms. Having an FFL and being an SOT does NOT exempt you from following state laws. Some states have exemptions for certain FFLs, but not all.

You must ensure that the states you're traveling through, and to, permit those certain firearms. If you're traveling to demo an NFA firearm for a government entity (law enforcement agency), a safe bet is to ship the NFA firearms to the agency in advance so that you don't need to travel with them.

NFA Transfers

An NFA transfer is whenever an NFA firearm is transferred from one taxpayer to another taxpayer. For example, when your business transfers an NFA firearm to another business (FFL), to an entity that's exempt from an FFL such as government agencies, or to a non-FFL taxpayer (your regular non-FFL customers).

Prior to each of these transfers, you must submit an application on the appropriate NFA Form and then wait for ATF approval before transferring the NFA Firearm.

The intended recipient must fill out the application, as it is their application for permission to possess the NFA firearm, and pay the associated tax (if any). You must retain possession of the NFA firearm even after they've paid for it and initiated the transfer process and not give the intended recipient possession of the item (away from your control) until they've received approval from the ATF in the form of their own tax stamp for that item. Remember, the ATF generally cares about possession and not ownership.

If you're a Class 2 SOT with a Type 7 manufacturer's FFL and you've made an NFA firearm, then you only need to notify the ATF that you've made the firearm. No permission is needed because an item in the NFRTR is not changing hands. Instead, you are letting them know to put the item in their database, the NFRTR, in the first place.

How to Transfer

How to transfer NFA firearms is a complicated enough topic to be covered in its own course. There are MANY things to consider therefore this SOT registration guide only covers the basics, and our ATF Compliance program covers it extensively.

For example, there are special rules and considerations for:

- transfer to trusts,
- transfers through estates to heirs of a will,
- documents and materials needed for non-FFL (normal customer) transfers,
- transfers to law enforcement agencies and individual law enforcement officers,
- pending transfers moved to a new FFL,
- repairs and returns to customers of NFA Firearms,
- how to remove a firearm from the NFR&TR (either through destruction or manufacture), and more

Transfers to Same EIN

If you are transferring an NFA firearm from one of your FFLs to another on of your FFLs, then it is not treated as a normal NFA transfer - instead, it is just like a transfer of a normal GCA firearm. This is because one taxpayer is not transferring the NFA firearm to another taxpayer. This means that you won't need to submit paperwork and wait for ATF approval before moving it to yourself at another FFL.

This is because the ATF sees your EIN as the same SOT. For example, lets assume you have one Type 1 FFL for your range and another Type 1 FFL for your retail store. If you have an NFA firearm on your retail store FFL and you want to transfer it to your FFL for the range, you can just log it out of your retail store's A&D record and then log it into your range's A&D record.

The ATF has asked that you submit a Form 5 notifying them that the NFA firearm has moved locations so that they may update its location in their NFRTR. Even if you tried to submit the Form 5, the ATF typically rejects it because you'd essentially be asking for permission to transfer it to yourself (even though they've said to do it). There is a method to protect yourself, notify the ATF without getting back a rejected Form 5, and bogging down their backlog of NFA forms. This is discussed in the follow-on ATF Compliance program.

Remember, the ATF doesn't see your status as an SOT by FFL number. They see it as you as an SOT being the proper possessor of that NFA firearm and as long as it stays with the same SOT (EIN), then it isn't an NFA transfer.

NFA Forms

Each of the ATF "Forms" are all technically Form 5320 with a different number after the decimal point. The number after the decimal point is where each form gets its nickname – "Form 1" is 5320.1, "Form 2" is 5320.2, and so on.

Same as with transfers in the previous lesson, the very basics are covered here. If you want to delve more into the forms, including how and when to use each, you'll need to join the ATF Compliance program.

Form 1

This form doesn't apply to FFLs. It is used by non-FFLs to make an NFA firearm. If you're interested in this form, you can read my article on ATF's NFA Form 1.

Form 2

This form is for Type 7 manufacturer FFLs to make an NFA firearm. This form is submitted AFTER the NFA firearm is made as a notification to the ATF (no approval required).

Form 3

This form is used to transfer NFA firearms from one FFL to another.

Form 4

This form is used to transfer NFA firearms from an FFL to a non-FFL (normal customer).

Form 5

This form is used for tax-exempt transfers of NFA Firearms such as transfers of unserviceable firearms, transfers to government entities, transfers to lawful heirs, and more.

About the author

Ryan Cleckner was born in Phoenix, AZ where he grew up hunting, shooting, and learning to love the outdoors.

Ryan served in the US Army's 1st Ranger Battalion of the 75th Ranger Regiment and he graduated from the premier sniper training program, the Special Operations Target Interdiction Course (SOTIC). He first deployed as a sniper, and then later as a sniper team leader, in support of the Global War on Terror in Afghanistan.

Ryan is an attorney that specializes in firearms law and has been involved in many parts of the firearms industry. He managed federal government affairs for the firearm industry's trade association, the NSSF, he was a SAAMI board member, a Vice President of Remington Outdoor Company, he created RocketFFL to help FFLs stay out of trouble with the ATF, and he co-founded GunUniversity.com and a free firearm compliance software company, FFLSafe.

Ryan has a passion for teaching - he has taught Constitutional Law at the University of Alabama in Huntsville and he has numerous online videos and articles sharing his passion for long range shooting online.

You can learn more about Ryan and contact him at his website, RyanCleckner.com

Made in United States
North Haven, CT
04 November 2026

21763968R00098